Gymnastics for Girls and Women

Gymnastics for Girls and Women

Linda Jean Carpenter

Parker Publishing Company, Inc.
West Nyack, New York

© 1985 by

PARKER PUBLISHING COMPANY, INC.

West Nyack, N.Y.

Library of Congress Cataloging in Publication Data

Carpenter, Linda Jean
  Gymnastics for Girls and women.

  Includes index.
  1. Gymnastics for women.   2. Gymnastics for women--
Study and teaching.   I. Title.
GV464.C29   1985   791.4′1′088042   84-19064

ISBN 0-13-371808-5

ISBN 0-13-371790-9 {PBK}

Printed in the United States of America

What this book offers you

Gymnastics creates joy through motion. Whether you teach, coach, or participate in gymnastics, you have a wonderful challenge.

Gymnastics for Girls and Women helps you use your own creativity and experience to produce a successful and enjoyable gymnastics program. This book is especially intended for you if you are a teacher of beginning and intermediate gymnastics classes or a coach of a gymnastics club or team starting competition. It will also be very useful to gymnasts themselves. It is not written for those seeking information on movements used only in a highly skilled, competitive team. This guide has been prepared with its intended audience constantly in mind; the problems of beginning or intermediate gymnasts are specifically addressed.

Before any gymnastics program can succeed, you need to prepare the gymnasium, the gymnast, and yourself. Chapter 1, *Preparing for Safety in Gymnastics*, gives you specific guidelines for equipment selection, location, and inspections; and it also discusses low-budget alternatives you can use to create more teaching stations. Chapter 3 gives you broad principles to follow in developing a conditioning and warm-up schedule for your gymnasts. The principles are based on physiological concepts of conditioning, and the warm-ups are designed for gymnastics. In addition, specific methodologies are presented for each area of the body needing conditioning or warming up for particular gymastics activities. As you prepare yourself for teaching or coaching gymnastics, consult Chapter 2, *Mechanical Principles*, and Chapter 6, *Effective Spotting*, for a detailed analysis of the skills you will need to evaluate movements, pinpoint errors, and spot efficiently. The chapter on spotting not only tells you how to spot traditional movements but also provides you with guidelines to use in developing spotting techniques for new movements as they arrive on the gymnastics scene.

Boredom and frustration are often problems in beginning and intermediate gymnastics programs. Some students advance quickly, while others learn at a slower pace. Adding variety to your program relieves the boredom of a gymnast who has quickly mastered a movement and also helps the gymnast who is still working on a movement. Chapters 4 and 5 give you a series of practical and specific suggestions for adding variety to your gymnastics program. Activities that teach gymnastics principles are presented; these activities involve stall bars, still rings, parallel bars, individual and dual stunts, self-testing activities, and even traveling rings.

The four Olympic events—floor exercise, balance beam, uneven parallel bars, and side-horse vaulting—are laid out in a manner that makes it easy for you to develop progressive lesson plans and unit plans. Each movement is set forth with headings such as:

Starting position
Procedure
Spotting
Common errors
Handy hints
Variations
Combinations

in language that is directed at both you and the performer. Many illustrations show correct performance techniques; other illustrations show common errors and spotting techniques. Chapter 11 gives you a full trampoline program, one that meets the guidelines of The American Alliance for Health, Physical Education, Recreation and Dance for use of the trampoline without inverted movements. Trampolining is valuable in development of the body awareness needed in gymnastics, and is also an end in itself. This book offers a progressive list of trampoline activities that give your gymnasts the benefit of trampoline experience without the expanded risk of inverted movements.

In many chapters you will find sample routines that incorporate varying combinations of the movements described in the chapter.

Finally, as your gymnasts reach the point in your program where it is appropriate to evaluate and grade them, you will find that Chapter 12 gives ideas for check-offs, grading systems, and even minimeet competitions for culminating activities.

In *Gymnastics for Girls and Women* you have everything you need to start and develop a complete gymnastics program for beginning and intermediate classes as well as for clubs and new teams.

Contents

1

Preparing for safety in gymnastics

The potential for serious injury is greater in any sport that involves the height, momentum, and body positions characteristic of gymnastics than it is in other sports. So attention to safety must also be greater. Competitive victories, easier teaching methods, and fulfillment of a gymnast's desire for a spectacular new skill should all be secondary to your concern for your gymnast's safety.

The United States Gymnastics Safety Association actively promotes gymnastics safety. Among its many safety programs and services is the certification of teachers and coaches in gymnastics safety.

To be effective, a safety program must be active rather than passive. Too many injuries occur because the teacher or coach fails to "think safety." Gymnastics itself is not unsafe. It is the *method* of participation rather than the sport that can make it unsafe. Safety does not just happen—it requires the participation of all involved.

The following questions should be resolved before *any* gymnastics participation occurs:

1. Is the equipment safe? Periodically inspect all the equipment and repair it as needed. The gymnastics equipment companies are generally better able to inspect ceiling mountings of rings and spotting belts than is the teacher. Keep a record of the inspection and its results on file both for legal purposes and as a reminder of when to conduct the inspection again.

1

The following checklist may provide ideas for you as you prepare your own checklist:

Mats

a. Check seams. If stitching is open, gymnasts can trip, and the mat's interior will deteriorate more quickly.

b. Check for soft spots and bottoming out. A worn mat may develop soft spots, which increase the risk of sprains. Select new mats carefully. Some of the less expensive mats are so soft that the gymnast's landing force is not absorbed but continues through to the floor.

c. Check corners for wear. Dragging wears out the corners, and then tears develop that can cause the gymnast to trip.

Equipment

a. Check for splinters, cracks, and gouges on wooden portions of equipment.

b. Check all welds and connections, nuts and bolts, and turn buckles.

c. Check for tightness of T-handles and other adjustment mechanisms.

d. Check for condition of protective mats, such as the mat on trampoline frames.

Spotting Belts

a. Check security of buckles, stitching, and rope attachments.

b. Check the suspension of overhead belts.

2. Is the location of the equipment safe? Unless you have a "perfect" gymnasium, you will probably have to be creative in setting out the equipment in order to get the most effective and safe use of floor space. As you review your gym, check what mat hooks, net hooks, wires, doors, and so forth could possibly injure a gymnast who lost all control. Be pessimistic in your considerations. Consider the space requirements of each type of equipment. For instance, the vaulting horse needs a long, narrow space. Several horses could safely be put quite close side by side. However, a long, unobstructed landing area is needed as well as an approach without cross traffic. The momentum pattern for the trampoline is less predictable than that of other pieces of equipment. *For this reason the trampoline should be located with plenty of room on all sides.*

3. Are emergency procedures set up to deal effectively with any emergency that might occur? Procedures to handle an injury must be established *before* the injury occurs.

    a. Post emergency numbers conspicuously for ambulance, fire, police, and team doctor (if you have one) or trainer or emergency health office. If the only phone within quick and easy access is a pay phone, it might be wise to keep some change somewhere nearby where it won't disappear.

    b. Have an appropriately stocked first aid kit available and know how to use it.

4. Is there any way to decrease the risk by altering the teaching progression? Many gymnastics skills can be more effectively and safely taught by teaching the separate components of the skill first. Many of the skills presented later in this book will include ideas for progressions.

Inherent in the use of progressions is the acknowledgment that some skills have necessary prerequisites. It is a mistake to allow an eager gymnast to attempt to learn a skill for which she lacks vital prerequisites. This practice both increases the risk of injury and introduces movement patterns that are difficult to correct later.

When you are considering progressions, remember that many skills fit easily into one or more of several categories. Examples are inverted skills, twisting skills, rotational skills, and kips. As you become familiar with several skills in one category, it becomes easier to develop progressions for others within the same category.

5. Is there any way to use padding, work lower, or use a spotting belt to decrease the risk? It is axiomatic that as a gymnast learns a skill she will make fewer and fewer mistakes. Since the majority of her mistakes are made at the early stages of learning, it is logical to try to create a situation where those mistakes hurt less, both physiologically and psychologically.

    a. Using Padding. When you think of padding, remember that you have two choices: Pad the equipment, or pad the gymnast. For instance, tubelike pads are available that fit tightly around the rail of the unevens. There are diaper-type hip pads for the gymnast who is learning skills on the unevens that involve heavy hip contact. Homemade alternatives also exist, such as towels taped around the bar, towels taped around shins likely to be bruised in squat mounts, and sweat shirts with padding sewn down the back to make a softer landing for the gymnast doing a forward roll on the beam.

b. Working Lower. Balance beam skills often lend themselves to practice on the floor first or at least on a lowered beam. The uneven rails can also be lowered. Height increases risk.

c. Using a Spotting Belt. The use of a hand spotting belt provides a surer spot for many skills. Overhead spotting belts are of great assistance, particularly in trampoline work, but the teacher must practice using the belt before the gymnast tries a new skill in it.

6. Is the gymnast physiologically ready? What strengths or flexibilities are needed for the skill? Does the gymnast have these requirements, or does she first need to complete a conditioning program for this skill's specific requirements?

The lack of strength required for a skill endangers the gymnast's safety. It also handicaps the learning process and often forces her to develop incorrect, alternative movement patterns that may cause a further delay in the learning process.

The lack of flexibility is a more obvious danger to the gymnast. Pulled or torn muscles can often be easily avoided by considering all aspects of the flexibility requirements of a skill before it is taught. Warm-ups may also need to be considered for the specific flexibility required.

7. Is the gymnast psychologically ready? The gymnast must trust her own capability to perform in addition to trusting your judgment and skill in teaching and spotting. The gymnast must also understand the risks involved in a particular skill in order to effectively develop a positive trust. A trust without knowledge is unlikely to continue.

When the gymnast attempts a new skill and it does not go well or she misses on an old skill, she may not be psychologically ready to try again without some practice on earlier steps in the learning progression. The idea that when one falls off a horse the best cure is to get back on may be entirely inappropriate for your gymnast.

8. Is the gymnast cognitively ready? Does the gymnast intellectually understand what is involved in the skill being taught, that is, head position, grip, timing, and so forth? It is also important to be sure that what you understand to be the portion of the skill to be practiced is the same as what the gymnast understands.

9. Does the spotter understand the skill and its common errors?
The same cognitive understanding necessary for the gymnast is also necessary for the spotter. In addition, the spotter is better prepared if she/he understands the common errors and how to deal with them. Common errors are included for many of the skills presented in this book.

10. Is the spotter physically capable of providing an adequate spot? Some movements require a spotter with a good deal of strength. The gymnast is done a disservice when her spotter fails to acknowledge the need for a second or stronger spotter. Some movements do not actually require two spotters, but the addition of a second spotter places less of a burden on the first.

The body type of the spotter is sometimes important, too. A tall spotter may be needed for some skills. If a taller spotter is unavailable, a shorter spotter can stack mats upon which to stand. A spotter should never stand on a chair, table, or other support that could injure a falling gymnast or spotter.

Jewelry on the spotter is just as dangerous as jewelry on the gymnast.

GENERAL SAFETY RULES

Make the safety rules an integral part of every gymnastics experience. Follow the rules yourself, and always insist that your gymnasts also follow them.

The following list, prepared by the United States Gymnastics Safety Association, presents the more commonly stressed rules:

1. Caution: Any activity involving motion, rotation, or height may cause serious accidental injury.
2. Do not use apparatus without qualified supervision.
3. Wear proper attire and use chalk when necessary to prevent slipping.
4. Before mounting apparatus, make sure it is properly adjusted and secured, and that sufficient mats, appropriate to the exercise, are in position. Consult your instructor.

5. Use proper conditioning and warm-up exercises before attempting new and/or vigorous moves.

6. Attempt new skills in proper progression. Consult your instructor.

7. When attempting a new or difficult skill, a qualified spotter should be used. When in doubt, always use a spotter—check with your instructor first.

8. Dismounts from apparatus require proper landing techniques. Do not land on head or back as serious injury may result. Consult your instructor.

9. Any skill involving the inversion of the body could be dangerous and cause serious neck or head injury.

10. "No Horse Play" at any time while on or around the gymnastics equipment.

2

Mechanical principles of gymnastics

There are basic mechanical principles that are common to many gymnastics skills. The gymnast who develops a physical as well as cognitive understanding of these principles is likely to learn more easily, and corrections of errors are usually more effective when based on mechanical principles.

TERMS FOR MAJOR GYMNASTICS MUSCLE ACTIONS

Specific terms exist for specific muscle actions. Examples of these are *flexion, extension, abduction,* and *adduction.* Without the use of these specific terms, there can sometimes be confusion in what seems to be a simple statement, like "point your toes." "Point your toes" is often alternately interpreted by the uninitiated as: lifting toes up or contracting the sole of the foot so that the toes point downward. Neither interpretation is appropriate for gymnastics. What is really meant is an action called plantar flexion, which affects the ankle joint, plus flexion of the toes. Plantar flexion means moving the ball of the foot toward the floor (Figure 2-1a).

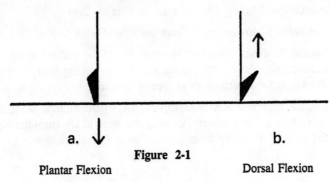

a.   b.

Figure 2-1

Plantar Flexion   Dorsal Flexion

7

Dorsal Flexion means moving the ball of the foot away from the floor (Figure 2-1b).

Other common actions in gymnastics are:

Flexion: Decreasing the angle between two bones (Figure 2-2).

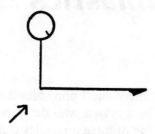

a. Hip Flexion

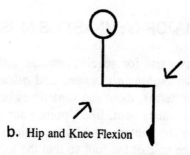

b. Hip and Knee Flexion

Figure 2-2

Extension: Increasing the angle between two bones (Figure 2-3).

Adduction: Moving toward midline (Figure 2-4).

Abduction: Moving away from midline (Figure 2-5).

Medial (Internal) Rotation: Moving toward the midline along the longitudinal axis. For example, rotating the straight leg from the hip so that the knees face each other is medial rotation.

Lateral (External) Rotation: Moving away from midline along the longitudinal axis. For example, rotating the straight leg from the hip so that the knees face away from each other is lateral rotation.

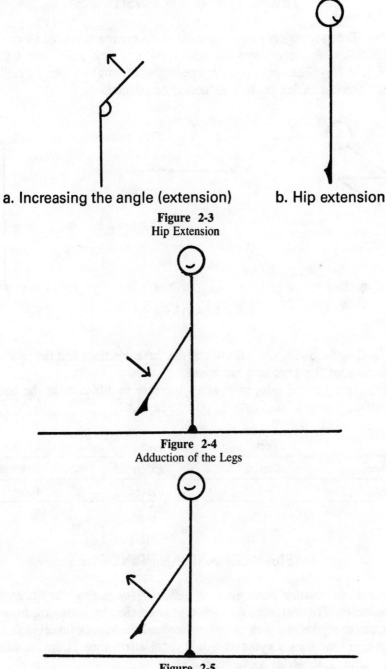

a. Increasing the angle (extension)   **b. Hip extension**

Figure 2-3
Hip Extension

Figure 2-4
Adduction of the Legs

Figure 2-5
Adduction of the Legs

TERMS FOR BODY POSITIONS

The vast majority of gymnastics skills are characterized by one of the following three terms for body position: *tuck, pike,* and *layout* (Figure 2-6). The application of one of these terms to a specific skill is independent of leg or arm abduction or adduction.

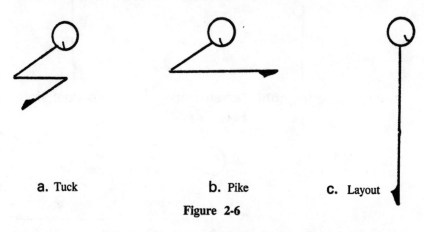

a. Tuck   b. Pike   c. Layout

Figure 2-6

The following chart illustrates the three positions and the relative function of the knee and hip joints.

As a general rule, most skills increase in difficulty as the body position changes from tuck to pike to layout.

	Tuck	Pike	Layout
Knees	Flexed	Extended	Extended
Hips	Flexed	Flexed	Extended

BASIC MECHANICAL PRINCIPLES

1. In rotation movements, the shorter the radius, the faster the rotation. For instance, the radius is decreased by changing from a layout to a pike to a tuck position (Figure 2-7). A tuck involves faster rotation (and thus a gymnast would require less time in the air when performing an aerial movement).

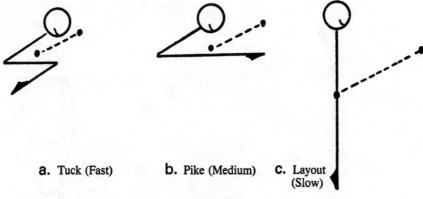

a. Tuck (Fast)   b. Pike (Medium)   c. Layout
(Slow)

Figure 2-7

2. Asymmetry of body parts produces unwanted rotation. If the legs or arms are not maintained in a symmetrical position, an unwanted twist is likely to enter into a movement that involves forward or backward rotation. So, whenever your gymnast has an off-balance ending to a skill that involves forward or backward rotation, consider the possibility that she is turning her head, dropping a shoulder, lifting one arm, and so on.

The symmetry of body parts is critical to many skills. You might find it helpful to have your beginning students learn this principle clearly by performing the following four skills (all of which become off-balance if asymmetry occurs):

a. Half twist on floor (180°)—watch for torso bending.
b. Full twist on floor (360°)—watch for dropped arm.
c. Standing pivot on beam—watch for dropped arm or shoulder.
d. Half twist on uneven bars (long hang from high bar)—watch for one-leg abduction.

3. Alignment of body parts increases balance in inverted movements. If we look at handstands from the side, we are likely to see an alignment of body parts similar to either *a* or *b* (in Figure 2-8).

The hands are obviously the base of support. In order to maintain forward–backward balance, body parts must be equally distributed in relation to a line drawn vertically through the hands. Figure 2–8*a* shows the correct alignment, with the line passing through the shoulders, hips, and feet.

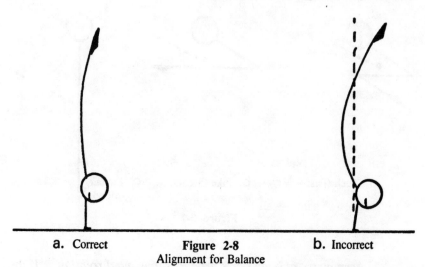

a. Correct   **Figure 2-8**   **b.** Incorrect
Alignment for Balance

Let's examine the component parts of the incorrect handstand in Figure 2–8. The first problem is found at the shoulder joint. If the rest of the body is vertical, as in Figure 2–9a, it is apparent that the gymnast would be overbalanced and fall. The gymnast's body seems to know this and thus tries to compensate by putting the hips on the other side of the vertical line (Figure 2–9b).

If Figure 2–9b represented all the compensation done, the gymnast would be underbalanced and fall. So the "knowing" body makes one final compensation. It arches the back so that the feet are on the overbalanced side (Figure 2–9c).

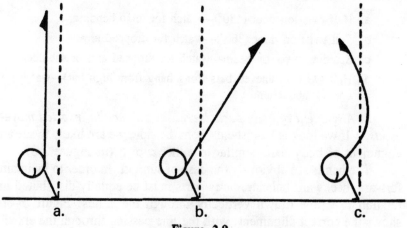

a.   b.   c.

Figure 2-9
Handstand Alignment

Many years ago, an arched handstand similar to that in Figure 2-9c was preferred. The arched handstand compensates somewhat for deficiencies in the gymnast, such as inflexible shoulders and poor control. (The arched handstand lowers the center of gravity a bit.) But it is improper form by today's standards and is also an inhibiting factor in using the inverted position to build other movements, such as the handspring.

Two simple skills that you might want to have your students experiment with to develop an understanding of the need for alignment are:

1. Inverted hand—stall bars.
2. Inverted hand—rings.

3

Preparing the gymnast

Flexibility, strength, and cardiovascular endurance are the three most important physiological factors to be considered in preparing the gymnastics student. A lack of preparedness in any of these three areas is likely to inhibit the student as she tries to move through the optimal motor pattern for the skill she is learning.

Most exercises are included in a gymnastics program for one of two reasons:

1. To condition for future days of practice
2. To warm-up for today's practice

Although the activities used in conditioning and warm-up programs may be identical, the principles behind their selection must be considered carefully.

CONDITIONING

The human body makes amazingly fast progress in a conditioning program, but you must plan ahead.

Flexibility

Flexibility, or the ability of a joint to move through an entire range of motion, is a critical quality to be developed in gymnasts—competitor and student alike.

Flexibility is very specific to the joint involved. There is no reason to assume that flexibility in one area of the body makes flexibility in another area more likely. For example, a gymnast who can perform splits with great ease may have a particularly inflexible back. *Therefore, design programs that develop flexibility in all areas of the body.*

15

Generally, flexibility exercises are divided into two types: phasic and static. Phasic exercises include ballistic, or "bobbing" type, exercises, such as toe touching with rhythmical up-and-down action. Static exercises may best be described as stretching a muscle until the stretch pain is reached, then holding that stretch pain position for a period of time without motion. In the long run, static exercises produce as much or more flexibility than phasic. Phasic exercises will produce a larger increase in flexibility on the day they are performed, but they may also produce more discomfort the following day because of small muscle tears. The knowledgeable teacher generally *avoids the use of phasic exercises* in conditioning programs. If an immediate flexibility is needed for some reason, slow phasic exercises are more prudent than fast bobbing.

Avoid two-person flexibility exercises. Using one student to pull, push, or simply apply weight to another's flexibility exercises is inviting excessive stretch.

Each movable joint in the body is capable of increased flexibility. However, for a gymnast there are six areas of the body that must frequently demonstrate an increased range of motion: hamstrings, leg adductors, hip flexors, ankle dorsaflexors, lumbar region of the back, and shoulders. In order to increase flexibility in any of these six areas, the muscles inhibiting the range of motion should be identified and then put on stretch according to the principles relating to flexibility.

Hamstrings: Hamstring flexibility is necessary for any deep pike position. The hamstring area seems to be the region most frequently stretched in the search for flexibility. Women benefit more from hamstring exercises if the feet are a few inches apart during the stretching. It is also important to remember the *hazard of hyperextension of the knee* (pushing the knee backward beyond its normal range of extension, thus weakening the knee joint). Hyperextension of the knee is more common in standing hamstring stretches than in sitting ones. Figure 3-1 through 3-5 show a few examples of hamstring stretching exercises.

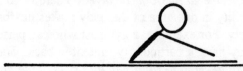

Figure 3-1 Hamstring Stretch
Feet a few inches apart.

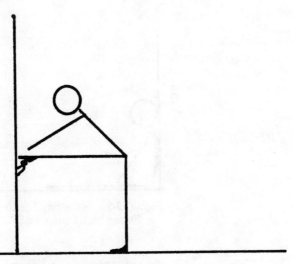

Figure 3-2 Hamstring Stretch
Bar/Wall Stretch.

Figure 3-3 Hamstring Stretch
Lift hips and straighten knees to "stretch pain."

Figure 3-4 Hamstring Stretch
Loop towel around instep of foot and pull.

Figure 3-5   Hamstring Stretch
Flatten back against wall.

Hip flexors: When the hip flexors contract, they allow us to pike. The hip flexors lack flexibility in a great many students. Most students who have a sway back (lordosis) also have inflexible hip flexors. Flexibility of the hip flexors is vital in the performance of splits, as well as other movements. Examples of exercises to develop flexibility in the hip flexors are found in Figures 3-6 through 3-8.

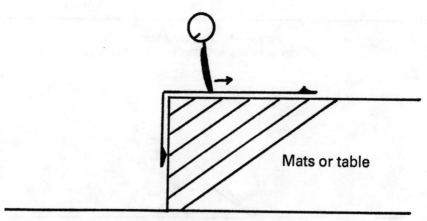

Figure 3-6   Hip Flexor Stretch
Tilt pelvis backward to stretch pain.

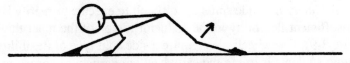

Figure 3-7 Hip Flexor Stretch
Hand supported stretch—try to straighten back leg.

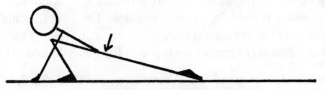

Figure 3-8 Hip Flexor Stretch
Deep lunge—pull pelvis toward floor.

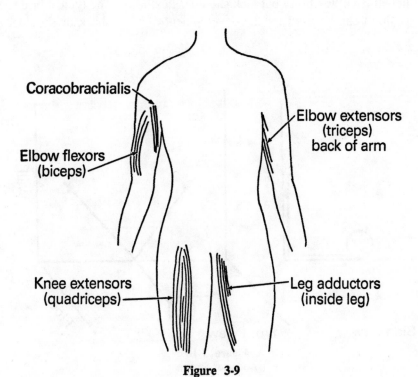

Figure 3-9

Adductors: Side splits are difficult to execute primarily because of insufficient flexibility in the adductor region of the inner thigh (see Figure 3-9). Cartwheels also require a side split type of flexibility. Beginning students learning the cartwheel are particularly prone to small muscle tears in the adductor region due to insufficient flexibility in this area. A simple static exercise is amazingly effective in the conditioning of this area (See Figure 3-10). The gymnast, while lying on the floor with her legs up against the wall, slides the hips as close to the wall as possible. The pull of gravity provides a sufficient stretch if the static position is held for several minutes. The knees should remain extended, and the gymnast should concentrate on relaxing the adductor region. Additional examples are found in Figures 3-11 and 3-12, p. 21.

Ankle dorsaflexors: A gymnast can work on the flexibility of ankle dorsaflexors by assuming a kneeling position with the tops of the feet on the floor. Bring the body down to sit on the feet.

Back and shoulder flexibility: Most female gymnasts have sufficient back flexibility but lack shoulder flexibility. The typical bridge position can be used for the development of either back or shoulder

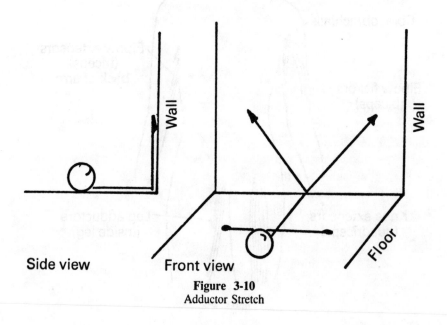

Side view   Front view

Figure 3-10
Adductor Stretch

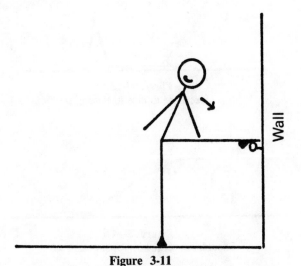

Figure 3-11
Adductor Stretch
Stand with one shoulder closer to bar. Pull shoulder toward bar.

Figure 3-12
Yoga adductor stretch—pull chest toward feet.

flexibility. It is important to feel the stretch pain in the shoulders and not only in the lumbar region of the back. The portion of the shoulder that will be stretched is the coraco-brachialis portion (Figure 3-9). Unlike the other exercises previously discussed the bridge is an exercise that some students may find difficult to perform initially. If this is the case, another student in the class can assist the student who is having trouble. Once the starting position is attained (Figure 3-13), the spotter stands at the performer's side and places the hand closest to the performer's head under the shoulders. The other hand reaches over and prepares to lift the hips. As the performer attempts to straighten her elbows and knees, the spotter *gently* lifts. Do not force the gymnast farther than her flexibility easily allows. When sufficient flexibility has been gained, the complete bridge should look like Figure 3-14.

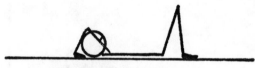

Figure 3-13
Bridge—feet close to hips in starting position.

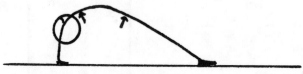

Figure 3-14
Shoulders over hands—spot at arrows.

Shoulders: Insufficient shoulder flexibility inhibits the correct performance of almost all inverted movements. Tight shoulders are characterized in the handstand position by too much back arch or by the shoulders being located in front of the hands instead of directly over them (Figure 3-15). Examples of exercises for the shoulders are found in Figures 3-16 through 3-18.

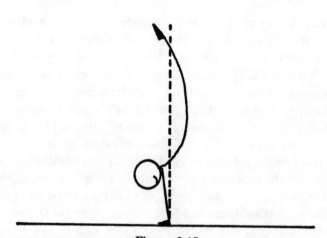

Figure 3-15
Handstand alignment with inflexible shoulders.

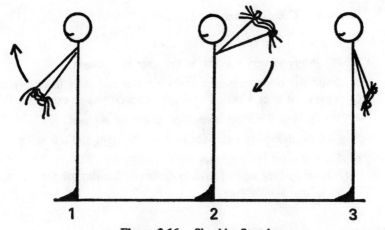

1   2   3

Figure 3-16 Shoulder Stretch
Keep elbows straight; move towel front to back.

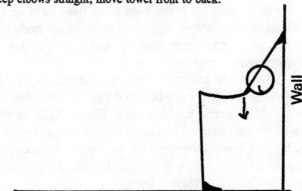

Figure 3-17
Wall stretch—pull shoulders toward floor.

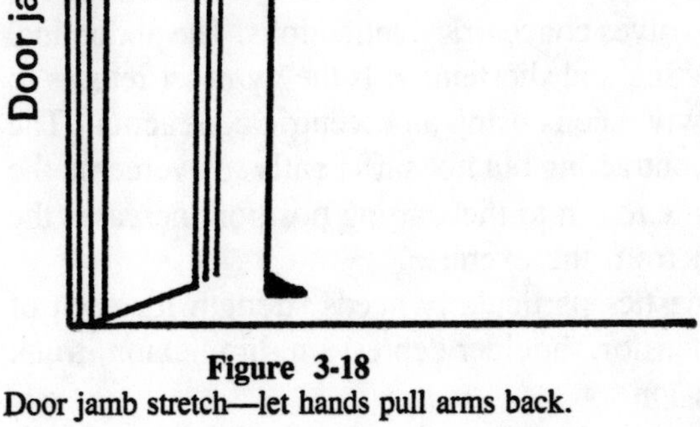

Figure 3-18
Door jamb stretch—let hands pull arms back.

Summary: Conditioning for Flexibility

1. Conditioning takes time. Plan ahead.
2. Flexibility is very specific to the joint in question.
3. Static flexibility exercises provide better and safer flexibility improvement over a period of weeks than do phasic exercises.
4. Two-person flexibility exercises should be avoided.
5. Perform flexibility exercises on both the right and left sides.
6. The six most critical areas for flexibility are:
   hamstrings, leg adductors, hip flexors, ankle dorsaflexors, lumbar back, and shoulders.

Strength

A gymnastics participant must have sufficient strength, power, and muscle endurance in several areas of her body to allow her to perform correct movement patterns and to provide her with a reserve for coping with mistakes.

When one contracts a muscle, the muscle tries to become shorter, and therefore the bones attached to it move closer together (except in static or eccentric contractions). This is called a concentric contraction. An eccentric contraction occurs when a muscle contracts with insufficient force to overcome the force of gravity or other external forces so that, as it is trying to shorten, the muscle is, in fact, being forced into a lengthened position.

Eccentric contractions, sometimes called negative work, have been shown to be capable of producing greater strength gains than concentric contractions. *Therefore, the gymnast who wants to get the greatest benefit from her conditioning program should use both concentric and eccentric contractions effectively.* To illustrate how this may be accomplished, consider the familiar exercise called the sit-up. The sitting up portion involves concentric contractions: The abdominal muscles are both contracting and shortening. If the gymnast returns to her starting position slowly, she is using an eccentric contraction: The abdominal muscles are contracting but not sufficiently to overcome the force of gravity. The slow return to the starting position increases the gymnast's strength gain from the exercise.

A student of gymnastics particularly needs strength for each of the following: elbow extension/shoulder depression, hip flexion, trunk flexion, and knee extension.

Elbow extension/shoulder depression: The triceps muscles (back of upper arm) are notoriously weak among most females. In addition to prohibiting the gymnast from successfully completing many gymnastics skills, a lack of elbow extension strength places her in danger. The gymnast who cannot control her body weight on her arms will also be unable to save herself from many common errors. Some useful exercises for elbow extension/shoulder depression strength are found in Figures 3-19 through 3-23.

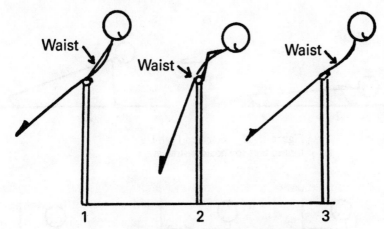

Waist   Waist   Waist

1   2   3

Figure 3-19   Vertical Push-Up
Bend elbows and bring waist to bar; extend elbows.

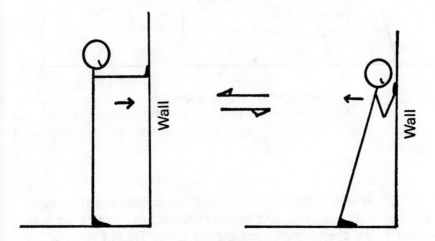

Wall   Wall

Figure 3-20   Wall Push-Up
Keep body straight.

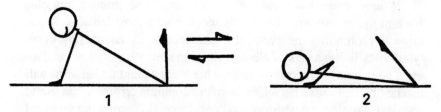

Figure 3-21   Modified Push-Up
Stay straight from shoulders to knees.

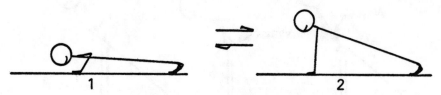

Figure 3-22   Standard Push-Up
Keep toes to shoulder straight.

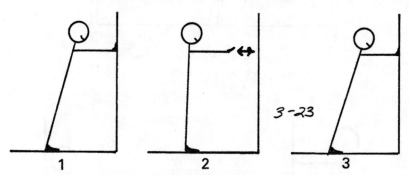

Figure 3-23   Wall Push-Away
Keep elbows straight; push from shoulders.

Hip flexion: Hip flexion and trunk flexion (abdominal strength) are frequently confused. Hip flexion is the act of bringing the legs closer to the chest without bending the torso. Trunk flexion is the curving or rounding of the back. Both are needed by the successful gymnast.

Many gymnasts have used leg lifts from the supine position to strengthen the hip flexors. Unfortunately, this common exercise generally does more harm than good. The lower back is usually slightly arched and tightened during this type of leg lift. This may lead to lower back pain. The danger of lower back pain is lessened if the leg lifts are performed in a standing or hanging position. Figures 3-24 and 3-25 provide examples of exercises to strengthen the hip flexors.

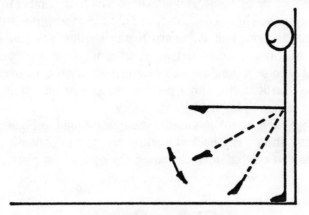

Figure 3-24 Standing Leg Lifts
Keep back flat against the wall.

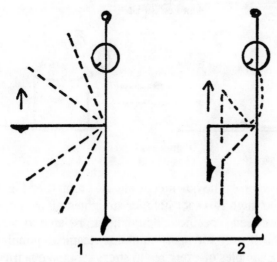

Figure 3-25 Hanging Leg Lifts
Start in long hand and lift legs together as high as possible. Hold and return slowly.

Trunk flexion: Sit-ups have long been the universal antidote for weak abdominal muscles. Unfortunately, this useful exercise is often performed incorrectly. If the back is kept straight during the sit-up, the hip flexors and lumbar back extensors will be strengthened rather than the abdominals. Lower back pain and lordosis may develop as a consequence of this error. *Sit-ups should be performed with a bent leg*. Also, if at all possible, sit-ups should be performed without anyone holding down the feet of the gymnast. It is also important to remember to round the back, bring the chin to the chest, and use the concentric as well as eccentric contraction; that is, return to the starting position slowly (Figure 3-26). Sit-ups are easiest when the arms are extended toward the feet and become more difficult when the arms are moved overhead. To increase the difficulty, either perform the sit-ups on a slant board (feet up) or add weights held by the hands.

Another exercise for abdominal strength is found in Figure 3-27. Move swiftly from sway-backed starting position to abdominal contraction phase. Look at stomach during the contraction phase.

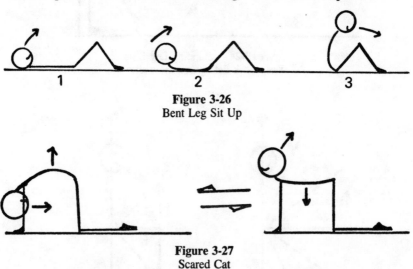

Figure 3-26
Bent Leg Sit Up

Figure 3-27
Scared Cat

Knee Extension: The quadriceps muscle group (See Figure 3-9) in the front of the thigh is responsible for straightening the knee. This group of muscles needs specific conditioning to be able to contribute effectively to the lift-off for many tumbling, leaping, jumping, and vaulting skills. Examples of exercises to strengthen the quadriceps are found in Figures 3-28 and 3-29.

Feather jumps, (fast, low jumps) can also be effective in increasing extension strength of the knee.

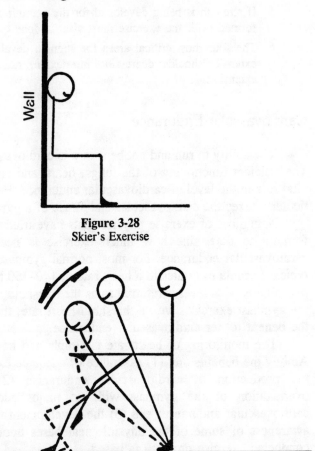

Figure 3-28
Skier's Exercise

Figure 3-29
Lunge Push-Away

Summary: Conditioning for Strength

1. Conditioning takes time. Plan ahead.

2. Females can improve strength markedly but, because of the lack of high levels of the hormone testosterone, seldom develop excessive muscle bulk.

3. Resistance, repetition, and rapidity may each be accentuated in order to develop the specific areas of strength, power, and muscle endurance.

4. The principle of overload (more resistance than the muscle is used to) is necessary to develop strength.

5. If strength is being developed for the execution of a quickly performed skill, the exercise must also be done quickly.

6. The four most critical areas for strength development are elbow extension/shoulder depression, hip flexion, trunk flexion, and knee extension.

Cardiovascular Endurance

The ability to run and not be weary is cardiovascular endurance. The efficient functioning of the lungs, heart, and circulation plays a vital role in the level of cardiovascular endurance. Floor exercise particularly taxes the cardiovascular endurance of a gymnastics student.

A number of exercise physiologists have tried to find a reliable formula to determine how much exercise is needed to increase cardiovascular endurance. For most normal gymnastics students, the typical formula translates to a heart rate of 140–150 beats of the heart per minute. This level is referred to as the threshold level. The longer the gymnast exercises with a threshold heart rate, the greater will be the benefit to her cardiovascular endurance.

The monitoring of heart rate is simple and has many benefits. Among the benefits are; (1) assurance of adequate exercise levels for the production of cardiovascular endurance; (2) avoidance of overtaxation of the gymnast with no major additional gain in cardiovascular endurance; and (3) the development of the gymnast's awareness of some of the physiological bases upon which a well-conducted exercise program is based.

Sample exercises are not included in this section because, in effect, almost any exercise that increases heart rate can be adapted to provide cardiovascular endurance. The adaptation involves the increase of rate and/or duration to levels that produce threshold heart rates. Frequently used exercises include some type of running or aerobic dancing.

Summary: Conditioning for Cardiovascular Endurance

1. Threshold heart rates must be reached for substantive increases in cardiovascular endurance.

2. The longer the participant exercises at a threshold level, the greater the benefit to cardiovascular endurance.

3. Through changes in rate and duration, most exercises can be used to produce cardiovascular endurance.

WARM-UPS

Unlike conditioning exercises, warm-ups are used to prepare the gymnast for activities to be performed immediately. Warm-ups are generally used to stretch out, increase body temperature, or acclimate the participant for the day's activities.

In selecting exercises for use as warm-ups, you need to consider:

1. Specificity: Select warm-ups that will provide the range of motion or increase the muscle temperatures in the specific areas to be used in the day's activities.

2. Intensity: The intensity of the warm-up exercise should be related to the conditioning level of the gymnast so as not to produce fatigue.

3. Duration: The warm-up activity should be continued for a length of time that is sufficient to increase muscle temperature but not cause fatigue.

4. Type: Selection of the type of warm-up (total body or only a localized area) should be related to the goals of the warm-up benefit needed.

4

Using auxiliary equipment for conditioning and progressive learning

Does your gymnasium have stall bars, still rings, or traveling rings? If it does, you have additional teaching or training stations for your gymnastics program. Since most of us wish we had more equipment, it is important to effectively use all the equipment we do have. Men's parallel bars and horizontal bars can be used to learn and practice uneven bar skills. Let us consider each type of auxiliary equipment separately and discuss some uses of each.

STALL BARS

The stall bars look rather "old-fashioned." However, the use of stall bars is a case of old fashion being good fashion. A variety of warm-up and conditioning skills can be performed on the stall bars. It is prudent to place mats under the stall bars for each of the following skills, particularly the inverted hang.

Long Hang

Starting position: Climb to a position with the hands on the top rung, back to the bars, body extended.

Procedure: Release the feet or heels from the bar and relax the entire body except the hands and neck. (Head should be erect.) Hold this position for at least 15 seconds.

Benefit: Static stretching of shoulders and general body relaxation.

Tuck Curl

Starting position: Long hang with back to the bars.

Procedure: Tuck knees toward chest. Then, if possible, curl trunk and lift hips off the bar. Hold as long as possible, preferably at least 15 seconds. Return to the starting position as slowly as possible. (Remember, negative/eccentric contractions build strength even faster.)

Benefit: Hip flexor strength; abdominal strength (if the hips are curled away from the bar); moderate grip strength.

Leg Lift

Starting position: Long hang with back to the bars.

Procedure: Pike and lift legs as high as possible. The minimum goal should be to lift the legs to a horizontal position. Hold as long as possible, preferably at least 15 seconds. Return to the starting position as slowly as possible. Once again, remember the value of eccentric contraction!

Benefit: Hip flexor strength; moderate grip strength.

Note: Your strongest students may be able to lift their legs to a nearly vertical position. If they can, have them add to this exercise by curling the trunk and lifting the hips from the bars. This gives them the added benefit of abdominal strength.

Pull-ups and Chin-ups

These commonly known exercises develop elbow flexion and arm extension. There is no feeling more helpless than to be asked to do a chin-up and find one's arms simply cannot flex at all. Using the stall bars rather than only a chinning bar or horizontal bar for chin-up or pull-ups provides an aid for your weaker students. Your weaker students can place their feet on the lower rungs of the stall bars and climb up to a flexed chin-up position. Then they remove or partially remove their feet. Most of your weaker students should be able to at least hold this flexed position. Although the strength gains will only be at the elbow angle of the exercise, a bit of a gain is better than a totally frustrated student.

Hamstring Stretcher

Starting position: Face the bars, grasp a bar at shoulder height with both hands, and place both feet on the bottom rung.

Procedure: Keep the knees straight and move the hands downward one rung at a time until the stretch pain is felt. Maintain this position for at least 15 seconds.

Benefit: Hamstring flexibility and moderate grip strength.

Inverted Hang

The inverted hang has the added benefit of being a lead-up for the handstand. Beginning students often have difficulty with the handstand because they do not know what the inverted position feels like. They are often fearful of kicking up too far when, in fact, they have not even reached a vertical position.

Starting position: Stand facing the bars.

Procedure: Bend over and move so that the upper back and head are resting against the bars. Lift the hands behind the hips and continue around with straight elbows until the hands can grasp a bar. Pike and pull the hips against the bars then lift the legs to a vertical position. The leg lift portion can be performed in either tuck (easy) or straight-legged (harder) positions. Hold the inverted position. Return to the starting position by piking while leaving the hips against the bar as long as possible. Coming down with one leg at a time provides for more control.

Spotting: Stand at the gymnast's side. Make sure her hands are on the same bar. Gently lift and guide the hips toward the bars. Once the beginning gymnast's torso is inverted, additional confidence can be given if the spotter places a hand under her shoulder.

Benefit: Lead-up for handstand; coordination; a sense of the inverted position.

STILL RINGS

The still rings are another piece of gymnastics-related equipment that you will probably have in your gymnasium. The use of the still rings provides another teaching and training station in addition to yielding positive benefits in the areas of grip strength, coordination, flexibility, arm strength, and familiarity with several body positions typical of gymnastics. As with the stall bars, mats should be placed under the still rings, especially for the basket and the inverted hang. When you place the mats, do not forget to be generous. A falling gymnast is not in control and may fall farther away from the apparatus than you expect. Therefore, place the mats so that you are certain the falling gymnast will always land entirely on the mat.

Long Hang

Starting position: Position the rings so that they are almost out of reach. Stretch and grab one ring with each hand.

Procedure: Bend the knees so that the body weight is removed from the feet. Relax the entire body except the hands and neck. (Head should be erect.) Hold this position for at least 15 seconds.

Benefit: Static stretching of shoulders; general body relaxation.

Kidney Crusher

Starting position: Stand underneath the rings, which are a little above head height. Grasp one ring in each hand.

Procedure: Keep the body straight from the shoulders to the feet; lean backwards as far as possible. Rotate clockwise around the centerpoint of the feet. Face forward throughout the rotation. Repeat.

Benefit: Side stretch; moderate back and shoulder stretch; moderate grip strength.

Note: For some reason, most students like this skill. Perhaps it is because of its rather gruesome name. In any case, your students will gain in flexibility and have fun at the same time-a good combination! The lower the rings are, the greater the stretch will be.

Basket

Starting position: With the rings shoulder height or lower, grasp one ring with each hand. Bend the knees until the elbows are straight.

Procedure: Tuck and lift at least one foot upward to the nearest ring. Place the instep firmly in the ring and do the same with the other leg. Lift the chin away from the chest and allow the body to follow backward until the previously tucked body is now arched. The abdomen should be pointing toward the floor when the basket position is achieved. Reverse the procedure to return to the starting position.

Spotting: Stand at the side of the gymnast. Place the arm nearest her back on her lower back or hips. At the same time place the other forearm under the gymnast's thighs. Assist the gymnast by gently lifting the hips and legs. A beginning gymnast may be more confident if the spotter continues to spot her as she turns over into the arched position. To give this "confidence" spot, place hands on the gymnast's waist both in front and in back. Prevent the gymnast from overarching by giving her abdomen some support. This is generally necessary only for the first attempt.

Benefit: Moderate back and shoulder flexibility; moderate abdominal strength; familiarity with different body positions.

Inverted Hang-Backward Rotation Approach

Starting position: Same as basket.

Procedure: Tuck and lift at least one foot upward to the nearest ring. Once in an inverted tuck position, slowly extend the legs upward, parallel to the ring cables. As the body extension continues, straighten the back and place the head in a neutral position. To aid in balancing, hold the rings tightly against the hips. Remember to use good form once in the inverted position. Reverse the procedure to return to the starting position.

Spotting: Follow the same procedure as that used in the basket until the inverted tuck position is attained. Then reach around the gymnast and grasp the ring on the far side with both hands (one arm on each side of gymnast).

Benefit: Lead-up for handstand; coordination; moderate grip strength; a familiarity with the inverted position.

Note: If you have both stall bars and still rings in your gymnasium, it is best to have your students attempt the inverted hang on the stall bars first. The rings tend to swing or sway a bit, and thus the gymnast faces a little more of a challenge in performing the inverted hang on the rings than on the stall bars.

Inverted Hang-Forward Rotation Approach

The forward rotation approach to the inverted hang is a little bit harder for most beginning students because it involves a strong piking action and cannot be done by "climbing" up one foot at a time. However, it offers additional benefits in return. The movement pattern of forcing the hips up during a strong pike is very important in bent-hip vaulting and in several other skills, such as shoot-through on bars and squat and straddle mounts on the beam.

Starting position: With the rings at torso height, grasp one ring with each hand. Bend over as the hands move backward, behind the hips. Straighten the elbows and continue bending over until the arms are close to the vertical.

Procedure: Jump and pike strongly as the hips are elevated and the head moves downward (rotation around shoulder joint). Once an inverted tuck or pike position is attained (pike is better), slowly extend the legs upward, parallel to the ring cables.

Spotting: Same as for inverted hang-backward rotation approach.

Benefit: Lead-up for handstand; coordination; moderate grip strength; familiarity with the inverted position; carry-over value of strong pike action.

TRAVELING RINGS

Traveling rings are a lot of fun. They are also quite a challenge for most beginning gymnasts. Although the variety of activities on the traveling rings is very limited, most gymnasts stay interested in the challenge. You may find it helpful to start with the rings low enough to be used while the gymnast's feet are on the floor. This will allow the gymnast to develop the correct movement pattern without having to worry about grip strength.

Starting position: Grasp one ring with one hand. Run toward the next ring and grasp it with the other hand as soon as it can be reached.

Procedure: Let the momentum of the initial run carry forward to the completion of the swing. The initial momentum should be accentuated by flexing the forward arm. As the momentum reverses, flex the back elbow and allow the forward arm to straighten. At the height of the backswing, release the grip of the back hand and reach forward to the next ring. Again, let the forward momentum carry to the completion of the swing while contracting the forward elbow. Then, as the momentum reverses, flex the back elbow and continue as before.

Spotting: Place a strip of mats underneath the rings and extend the strip beyond the first and last rings. Generally, no spotting is needed. However, some gymnasts may find it easier to concentrate on the correct movement sequence if someone moves alongside and reminds them.

Benefit: Grip strength; elbow flexion strength; coordination.

Note: Chalk and handguards may help your gymnast's hands from becoming sore. Most gymnasts find that the traveling rings are quite hard on the hands.

EVEN PARALLEL BARS

Most even parallel bars can be made into *un*even parallel bars with the use of a conversion kit. However, parallel bars have a lot to offer your program even if they cannot be made uneven.

For the following activities on the even parallel bars, adjust the bars to about shoulder width apart.

Pike-up

Starting position: Jump to a straight arm support position between the bars, one hand on each bar.

Procedure: Lift the hips upward and backward while piking the body. Hold position as long as possible.

Benefit: Hip flexor strength; shoulder flexor strength.

Leg Lift

Starting position: Same as pike-up.

Procedure: Lift the legs toward a horizontal position. Hold the position. Do not allow the hips to move backwards.

Benefit: Hip flexor strength; moderate shoulder extension strength (to maintain hip position).

Straddle Travel

Starting position: Same as pike-up and leg lift.

Procedure: Swing legs backward a bit, then swing them forward vigorously. Straddle them and place one calf, knee, or thigh on each bar. (The better gymnasts will be able to place the thighs on the bar initially.) If the thighs are not on the bar initially, the legs should be slid outward until the thighs are in position. Then lean forward and shift the hands to a position on the bar in front of each leg. Swing the legs backward and between the bars so that the starting position is regained. Repeat.

Coordination; hip flexor strength; elbow extension strength; hip extension strength.

Basket

This skill is performed in the same manner as the basket on the still rings. Be sure to have the hands grasping the bars from the outside.

Walking Variations

Traveling from one end of the bars to the other builds balance and elbow extension strength in the gymnast. She will learn the positive benefits of controlling and effectively using body swing.

1. Walk: From a straight arm support between the bars, shift one hand then the other toward the other end of the bars.
2. Tuck Walk: Perform this skill in the same manner as the walk but tuck the legs.

3. Stride walk: Perform this skill in the same manner as the walk except with each hand motion forward; also step forward with the leg on the same side and swing the opposite leg backward.

Many other variations can be developed. Some gymnasts enjoy the opportunity of creating their own walks.

Layout Swing

Starting position: Jump to a straight arm support position between the bars, one hand on each bar.

Procedure: Pike slightly and swing forward, then straighten the body and swing backward. Continue swinging forward and backward with a straight body. Try to increase the height of the swing. Your beginning gymnasts may have to be content initially with simply swinging from the hips until they develop shoulder flexion and extension strength.

Benefit: Shoulder flexion and extension strength; balance; coordination; elbow extension strength.

Note: This is a good lead-up for a cast on the uneven bars.

HORIZONTAL BAR AND SINGLE BAR FROM EVEN PARALLEL BARS

Any skill that can be performed on one bar of the unevens can be learned and practiced successfully on (1) a horizontal bar borrowed from the men's gymnastics program, or (2) one bar of an even parallel bar set with one bar removed. By using either the horizontal bar or the single bar of the even set, you gain an additional teaching and training station for such skills as leg circle, seat circle, back hip circle, front hip circle, and single- and double-legged shoot-throughs.

In this chapter we have looked at several types of auxiliary equipment that can be used to provide additional teaching stations for your gymnastics program. Don't underestimate the value of their use. The skills described can be of major importance to all your gymnasts, particularly your beginners.

5

Broadening the base with stunts and self-testing activities

How do you keep your gymnasts from being bored as they practice necessary, basic skills? How do you get your students to overcome an unwillingness to touch each other and develop into aggressive spotters? How can you teach, using movement, such abstract concepts as momentum, base of support, and alignment?

A good answer to these questions is: include stunts and self-testing activities in your gymnastics program. The word *stunt,* as used in this chapter, refers to an activity that involves a combination of balance, coordination, flexibility, agility, and strength to perform a skill that is complete in itself. Often the sole goal of a stunt is for the performer to present an affirmative answer, through action, to the question, "Can you do this?" Even when stunts and self-testing activities do have this singular goal for the participant, they can be very useful in a beginning-level gymnastics program.

Stunts and self-testing activities provide variety. For instance, a lot of beginners have trouble getting back to a standing position after a forward roll. This happens because, as beginners, they haven't yet mastered the idea of moving the center of gravity forward over their feet. The beginner could master this by repeatedly attempting a forward roll until she finally finds success. But beginners are likely to become both bored and frustrated in the process. Some of the stunts and self-testing activities in this chapter develop skills that involve the same techniques as those needed in the forward roll. So stunts and self-testing activities provide the beginner with a way to learn and practice one technique through a variety of activities.

Stunts and self-testing activities can be employed successfully in large classes, with all age levels. Often older students enjoy them even

43

more than younger ones. They are fun and challenging but are not usually considered "scary" by beginners. The students gain confidence, and they start to relax as they learn.

Some stunts involve two or more people. These stunts have the added benefit of getting your gymnasts used to touching each other. To be good spotters, your students need to be willing to touch. Through the use of dual stunts, your students will learn to depend on each other and not to hesitate to touch each other when necessary. The concept of good spotting seems simple, but in reality it is very difficult to train beginners to be aggressive spotters. The inclusion of dual stunts is almost magical in overcoming this problem.

The stunts and self-testing activities are presented in two categories: (1) individual and (2) dual/multiple stunts.

INDIVIDUAL STUNTS

Egg Sit

Start: Sit on floor; bend knees; place feet close to hips. Grasp right toes with right hand, left toes with left hand.

Then: Lean back a little so that feet come off the floor. Extend knees to a position of moderate stretch, with legs abducted. Hold this position, balancing on hips (Figure 5-1).

Benefit: Flexibility (hamstring); balance.

 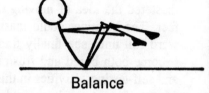

Start   Balance

Figure 5-1
Egg Sit

V-sit

Start: Sit on floor; bend knees; place feet close to hips. Place hands on floor behind body for balance.

Then: Lean back a little so that feet come off the floor. Extend knees completely while keeping the legs together (adducted). Extend ankles and hold the position (Figure 5-2).

Note: The body should form a "V," so try to maintain a reasonably straight back; for a bit more challenge put hands out to the side or up toward the toes.

Benefit: Flexibility (hamstrings); balance; hip flexor and abdominal strength. Develops understanding of correct gymnastics form for legs.

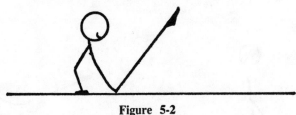

Figure 5-2
V-Sit

Knee Scale

Start: Kneel on floor on "all fours" with knees under hips and hands under shoulders.

Then: Extend one leg up and back; hold position (Figure 5-3).

Note: Keep elbows straight; lift head; don't let back sag.

Benefit: Balance; leg form control; coordination of body parts.

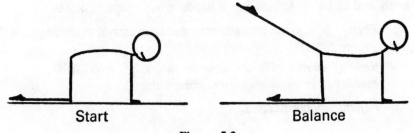

Start   Balance

Figure 5-3
Knee Scale

Front Scale

Start: Stand.

Then: Lift one leg backward, with knee extended. Keep supporting leg straight. When leg is as high as possible without putting shoulders forward, rotate leg around hip joint and allow leg to be lifted higher while lowering shoulders. Hold position (Figure 5-4).

Note: Keep the back arched and head up (cue: wrinkles in back of leotard). Don't sacrifice back arch for greater leg height. The body should form a half-moon position. Experiment with arm placement.

Benefit: Flexibility (hamstring); balance; coordination; form awareness.

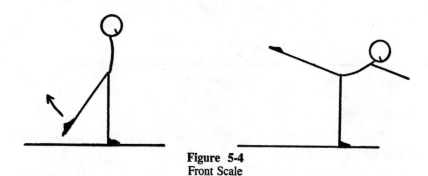

Figure 5-4
Front Scale

Egg Roll

Start: Kneel as close to the floor as possible, with buttocks on heels and chest on knees. Place hands around tops of knees.

Then: Roll to the side and continue until arrival at starting position (Figure 5-5).

Note: If several rolls are done in succession, alter depth of kneeling position to maintain a straight line.

Benefit: Coordination.

Figure 5-5
Egg Roll

Log Roll

Start: Prone position with arms extended overhead.

Then: Roll to the side and continue until arrival at starting position.

Note: If the legs are maintained in good form (adducted and extended), students will begin to understand the body control needed for twisting skills.

Benefit: Coordination; form development.

180° Spin

Start: Stand.

Then: Jump up and turn 180°; land with balance facing opposite direction.

Note: Accentuate symmetry of body parts (arms at same height, etc.) and insist on balance at landing. Balance and symmetry will add to student's mechanical understanding of twisting skills.

Benefit: Lead-up for twisting skill (such as swivel hips and pivot turns); coordination; balance.

360° Turn

Start: Stand.

Then: Same procedure as 180° turn, except that the turn is 360°.

Note: It will be very difficult to maintain balance upon landing without using correct twisting mechanics.

Benefit: Lead-up for twisting skills (such as swivel hips and pivot turns); coordination; balance.

Jump and Slap Heels

Start: Stand.

Then: Jump and, while in the air, slap heels with hands; land with balance (Figure 5-6).

Note: If you also add the requirement of landing softly, your students will learn about absorbing landing shocks by using the foot, ankle, knee, and hip.

Benefit: Leg extension strength; understanding of controlled-landing techniques; balance.

Figure 5-6
Jump and Slap Heels

Upswing

Start: Kneel on floor with torso vertical and toes tucked under.

Then: Shift weight backward and stand up, maintaining balance (Figure 5-7).

Benefit: Although this is a very easy stunt, it requires shifting of weight over the base of support for success. Balance; coordination; low-level lead-up for getting up from forward roll and similar skills.

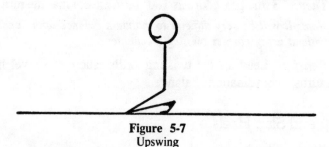

Figure 5-7
Upswing

Human Rocker/Roll Up

Needed: Mat.

Start: Supine; knees pulled toward chest; head pulled toward knees; hands grasp under thighs or around upper shins.

Then: Rock repeatedly from head to toe; place feet on floor with each forward rock; keep back rounded (Figure 5-8).

Figure 5-8
Human Rocker/Roll Up

Variation: Rock forward enough to place weight on feet and have hips come off floor for a moment.

Variation: With hands around upper shins, rock forward enough to place weight on feet and have hips come off floor for a moment, at which time, release grip on knees and clap hands under hips; then roll back.

Variation: Rock forward enough so that center of gravity is over feet; end in a balanced squat, or stand.

Benefit: Coordination; excellent lead-up for forward roll.

Inchworm

Start: Stand; bend over and place hands on floor about 2 or 3 feet in front of feet; straighten knees.

Then: Walk forward on the hands until a push-up position is achieved. Keep elbows straight as the feet walk up toward the hands, as close as flexibility allows. Repeat by walking hands forward (Figure 5-9).

Variation: When in push-up position, do one push-up and then continue.

Benefit: Flexibility (hamstring); arm extension strength.

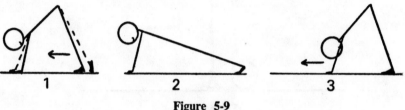

Figure 5-9
Inchworm

Crab Walk

Start: Sit on floor. Bend knees and place feet close to hips; place hands on floor a few inches behind.

Then: Lift hips off floor by pushing with straight arms and hip extensors. Walk in this position toward either feet or head (Figure 5-10).

Benefit: Hip extensor strength; leg extensor strength (quadriceps); coordination.

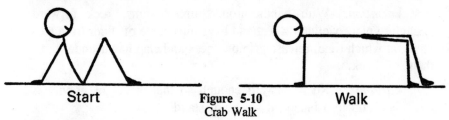

Start

Figure 5-10
Crab Walk

Walk

Shoulder Stand

Start: Supine.

Then: Pull knees toward chest; extend legs upward in a vertical plane; place hands on hips or lower back to support and balance; extend fully so that, from rib cage to toes, the body is in a vertical position without any pike; (Figure 5-11).

Benefit: Low-level lead-up for inverted skills, such as handstands, because it orients body about what is actually a vertical position. Hip extensor strength; form control; flexibility (neck), so thus a good warm-up for rolls.

Figure 5-11
Shoulder Stand

Bells

Start: Stand.

Then: Cross in front of right foot with left foot and step on left foot; kick right leg up to right; push off of left foot. While both feet are in the air click heels. Land on left foot. Then, to continue, cross in front of left foot with right, and so on, so that one heel click is done to the left and another to the right (Figure 5-12).

Benefit: Balance; coordination; leg extension strength.

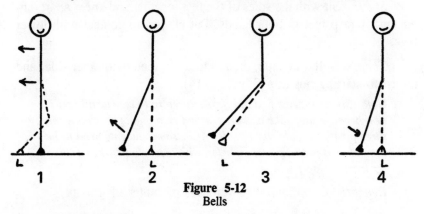

Figure 5-12
Bells

Turkish Sit-Stand

Start: Stand with feet crossed. Cross arms on chest.

Then: Sit gently on floor without uncrossing legs or arms. Return to standing position without uncrossing legs or arms; maintain balance (Figure 5-13).

Figure 5-13
Turkish Sit-Stand

Note: The secret of this stunt is to shift the center of gravity forward in order to return to the standing position.

Benefit: Low-level lead-up for forward roll (helps students having difficulty returning to a stand after forward roll); leg extension strength; balance; coordination.

Around the World

Start: Sit with the soles of the feet together and knees apart (abducted). Grasp feet in both hands. Put elbows in contact with lower legs.

Then: Roll onto side; then onto back; then onto other side, and return to starting position (Figure 5-14).

Note: Some students find it difficult to return to the starting position because they take a short cut and skip one of the following three positions: side, back, side. Also, some students need to be reminded to push against their leg with their elbow when getting up from a side position.

Benefit: Coordination; awareness of center of gravity.

Figure 5-14
Around the World

Tangle

Needed: Mats.

Start: Prone; bend knees and cross lower legs. Reach back with hands and grasp right toes with left hand and left toes with right hand.

Then: Roll side to side until you roll over arm and onto back. Rock forward onto hips and place feet on floor close to hips while still grasping toes. Continue rocking forward until center of gravity moves over feet. Stand up while still grasping feet. Place weight on back foot and guide forward foot with hand to side-by-side position. Release hands and stand erect with balance (Figure 5-15).

Benefit: Flexibility; balance; low-level lead-up to forward roll.

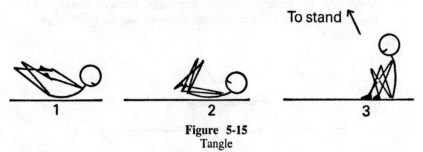

Figure 5-15
Tangle

Tip-Up

Needed: Mats.

Start: Squat with feet about 1 foot apart and knees apart. Place hands on floor about 1 foot apart, with fingers facing forward.

Then: Place elbow against leg just above knee; press elbows out and legs in; slowly rotate forward placing more and more weight on hands until no weight is left on feet; allow feet to leave floor and balance on hands (Figure 5-16).

Note: Weight should be shifted forward very slowly for balance.

Benefit: Low level lead-up for hand stand (become accustomed to weight on hands); arm strength; balance; coordination.

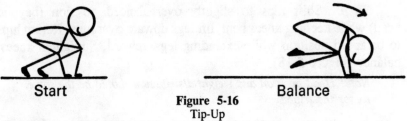

Start   Balance

Figure 5-16
Tip-Up

Tripod

Needed: Mats.

Start: Kneel; place hands on floor about 2 feet apart, with fingers pointing forward. Place forehead on floor about 1½ feet in front of hands.

Then: Walk forward with feet until the hips rise substantially and the feet are about 1–2 feet away from hands. Place knees on elbows; lift feet from floor; balance (Figure 5-17).

Note: Weight should be equally distributed between hands and head. (Weight on head is half on forehead and half just above forehead.)

Figure 5-17
Tripod

Precautions: A spotter can be used effectively to guide the student at the hips and also to prevent her from overbalancing. The spotter can stand or kneel by the inverted performer's back (or a bit to the side). Give your students sufficient mat space beyond them in case they overbalance.

Benefit: Lead-up for inverted skills, particularly the headstand; balance.

Headstand

Needed: Mats.

Start: Tripod position (preceding stunt).

Then: Shift hips to slightly overbalanced position (beyond head) while keeping knees bent; lift legs upward over hips. Return hips to balanced position while extending legs upward. Straighten knees; balance (Figure 5-18).

Note: Head position and weight distribution should be the same as for the tripod.

Precautions: Spotter should guide by placing hands on hips and prevent overbalancing; stand toward back (a bit to side) of inverted performer; provide ample mat space both in front and in back in case of overbalancing or underbalancing.

Benefit: Coordination; balance. May be used for lead-up for handstand, but remember that there are major mechanical differences.

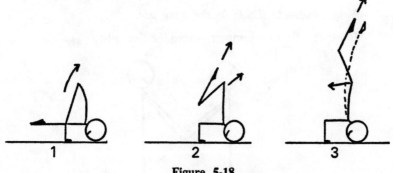

Figure 5-18
Headstand

DUAL AND MULTIPLE STUNTS

Back-to-Back Get-Up

Start: Sit with back touching back of partner. Bend knees and place feet on floor very close to hips. Reach backward and interlock elbows with partner.

Then: Push against partner's back and straighten legs until a standing position is reached by both performers (Figure 5-19).

Note: This is easier if performers are about the same size.

Benefit: Contact with partner; trust; leg strength.

Figure 5-19
Back-to-Back Get-Up

Wring the Dishcloth

Start: Stand facing partner; grasp partner's right hand with left and partner's left hand with right.

Then: Without letting go of hands, turn to the side and stand with backs together; continue turning until starting position is reached (Figure 5-20).

Note: Partners should be the same size.

Benefit: Partner contact, shoulder flexibility.

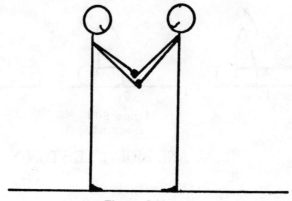

Figure 5-20
Wring the Dishcloth

Twister

Start: Stand facing partner. Take partner's right hand in your right hand.

Then: Lift left leg over connected right hands and turn back to partner; partner does same. Turn continues as right leg is lifted over partner's body; partner does same. End in starting position (Figure 5-21).

Benefit: Partner contact.

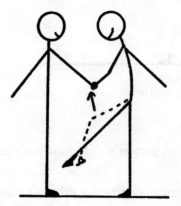

Figure 5-21
Twister

Rocker

Needed: Mats.

Start: Sit facing partner. With bent knees, place feet under partner's pelvis. Partner does same. Grasp partner's hands.

Then: Lean back and pull partner enough for her pelvis to leave floor; rock forward. Partner again sits on floor and then pulls. Repeat (Figure 5-22).

Variation: Scooter. Instead of returning to place, extend legs; partner extends knees even more on return to ground so that the two move down the mat.

Benefit: Partner contact; coordination.

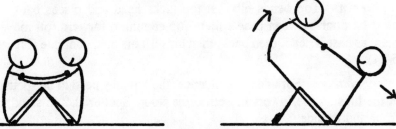

Figure 5-22
Rocker

Wheelbarrow

Start: One partner stands while other assumes a push-up position with elbows extended; first partner grasps the ankles of the other and lifts her legs.

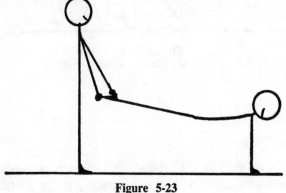

Figure 5-23
Wheelbarrow

Then: Move forward as a pair; one partner holding ankles of the other, other partner walking on hands and keeping back and legs extended (Figure 5-23).

Benefit: Partner contact; base-arm and torso strength.

Partner Forward Rolls

Needed: Mats.

Prerequisite: Forward roll.

Start: Base partner in supine position with knees bent and feet close to hips; top partner stands with feet next to base's shoulders and places hands on ankles of base. (Base's feet are about 1 foot apart.)

Then: Top bends elbows; top tucks head and places back of head on floor between base's feet. Top continues forward roll movement as base's head, then back, then hips lift off mat; continue (Figure 5-24).

Spotting: For added confidence, the top may need to be spotted at the hips as she lowers herself to the floor. Spotter should stand in front and to side.

Benefit: Partner contact; trust; confidence.

Figure 5-24
Partner Forward Rolls

Chest Stand

Needed: Mats.

Start: Base gets on "all fours" and prepares a sturdy base by having elbows extended, with hands directly under shoulders and knees a few inches apart and directly under hips. Top approaches base from side and places chest on base's back, with chin on far side of ribs; top reaches under base's rib cage and grips far side tightly.

Then: Top kicks one leg upward, followed quickly by other into a vertical position. Balance (Figure 5-25).

Spotting: Two spotters are best. One spotter stands near base's lower legs and helps lift top to vertical position. Second spotter stands on far-side of top and helps balance her legs and keep her from overbalancing.

Benefit: Partner contact; awareness that full weight of sister gymnast is manageable; lead-up for inverted skills (such as handstand); familiarity with inverted position.

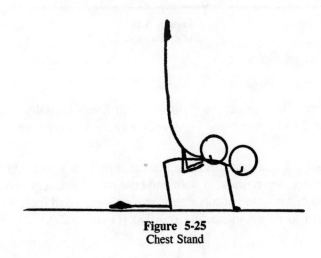

Figure 5-25
Chest Stand

Angel Balance

Needed: Mats.

Start: Base in supine position, with knees bent and feet close to hips; top stands facing base close to base's feet.

Then: Base lifts feet and places them on top's pelvis. (Top may need to lean forward a bit.) Base and top grasp hands; base counts to three, and on "three" base straightens legs upward and top pushes off floor into an extended horizontal position. Balance. Base decides when to return to starting position (Figure 5-26).

Spotting: Two spotters are best—one spotter on each side of top; extend arms under rib cage and thighs and assist in lifting and balancing.

Note: Top should be same size as base or smaller.

Benefit: Base—leg extensor strength; trust; partner contact. Top—leg and torso extensor strength; balance.

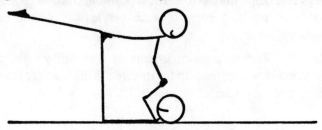

Figure 5-26
Angel Balance

Sitting Angel Balance

Needed: Mats.

Start: Base in supine position, with knees partially bent and feet about 2 feet above hips. Top stands with back to base, near base's feet.

Then: Top assumes a sitting position on base's feet. On base's count of three, top pushes off floor and base straightens legs vertically. Hold balanced position of top sitting on base's extended legs. Base decides when to return to starting position (Figure 5-27).

Figure 5-27
Sitting Angel Balance

Spotting: Two spotters are best. Spotters stand to each side of the base's feet and assist in lifting and balancing the top.

Note: Top should be same size as base or smaller.

Benefit: Base—leg extensor strength. Top—balance; partner contact; trust.

Horizontal Stand

Needed: Mats.

Start: Base in supine position, with knees bent and feet on floor close to hips. Top straddles base, facing base's feet and placing one hand firmly on each of base's knees. Top walks feet backward until base can comfortably grasp top's ankles.

Then: On base's count of three, base extends arms vertically while holding top's ankles; top pushes off floor and extends body horizontally (Figure 5-28).

Spotting: Two spotters are used; one spotter on each side of top with arms extended under top's thighs and hips to assist in lifting and balancing.

Note: This stunt works best if top is the same size as or smaller than the bottom.

Benefit: Arm extension strength for both top and base; torso extension strenth for top; balance; coordination; trust; partner contact.

Figure 5-28
Horizontal Stand

Triangle

Start: Same as wheelbarrow, except that base's ankles are placed on top's shoulders.

Then: Hold balanced position (Figure 5-29).

Benefit: Base—torso extension strength; low-level lead up to handstand since weight is borne on arms; contact.

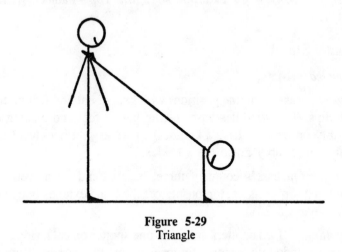

Figure 5-29
Triangle

The following stunts involve multiple participants. Besides the physical benefits of strength, balance, or coordination that are produced by these activities, they tend to develop a sense of class camaraderie. Class unity is always worthwhile, but particularly in gymnastics, where the students need to relieve tension and apprehension over new and sometimes "scary" skills.

Pyramids and Tableaus

Although the building of true pyramids with three or more layers of students is perhaps too hazardous, students can be encouraged to work in groups to perform tableaus using some of the static positions learned in the stunts section, and two-layer pyramids. You might want to suggest to students creating these tableaus that they consider the direction of the viewers, a set sequence for arriving at the ultimate tableau formation, and a set sequence for dismantling the tableau. A few samples are presented in Figures 5-30 through 5-32, but you will find that your students will be very creative.

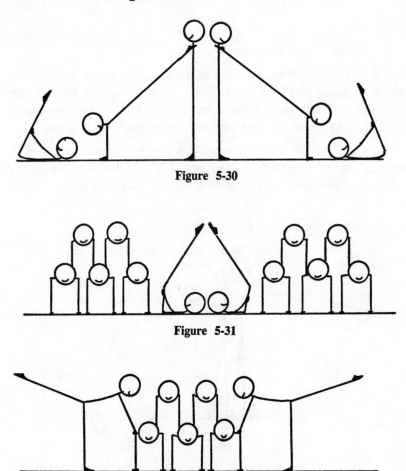

Figure 5-30

Figure 5-31

Figure 5-32

Walking Chair

Start: All participants stand very close together in single file and grasp the forearms of the person in front.

Then: Upon a signal from the last person in line, sit down on the thighs of the person behind, with knees bent no deeper than a right angle; last person in line then calls "left," "right," and all participants shuffle forward in cadence.

Benefit: Leg extensor strength; contact; trust.

Pinwheel

Needed:　Four participants at least.

Start:　Four gymnasts stand in a square, facing each other. One pair of opposite performers places their arms behind the necks of the other pair and grasps each other's arms; the other pair places their arms behind the backs of the first pair and grasps each other's arms.

Then:　All four begin to turn clockwise together. As momentum picks up, the first pair allows their legs to lift off the floor; the second pair continues to turn fast enough to keep the first pair in the air (Figure 5-33).

Benefit:　Partner contact; trust.

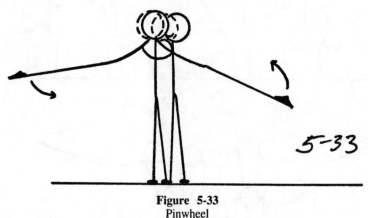

Figure 5-33
Pinwheel

Merry-Go-Round

Needed:　Mats; an even number of participants.

Start:　Suggest six or eight participants. Form a standing circle, with all participants holding hands. Every other person sits down and extends legs into center of circle so that her feet are in contact with other sitting participants.

Then:　Sitting participants extend and lift hips off floor, and at the same time the standing participants lean back a bit and start walking clockwise. Sitting participants take small, fast steps with their heels as the merry-go-round turns.

Benefit:　Contact; coordination.

6

Effective spotting

Effective spotting serves two critical purposes:

1. Protection from injury.
2. Assistance in performance.

Protection from injury is of paramount importance.

To be an effective spotter, one should consider each of the following elements:

1. Be aware of the skill to be spotted.   The gymnast and spotter need to communicate so that both are thinking of the same portion of the skill to be practiced. Problems in this area are often caused by an impulsive gymnast, a spotter who has spotted the same skill over and over until she is in a rut, or a gymnast who thinks the spotter is a mind reader.

One solution to this problem is to develop an empathy within the gymnast for the spotter's role. To do this, have all your gymnasts serve frequent turns as spotters. They will then develop an understanding that:

a. It is physically taxing to be a good spotter.

b. A spotter's role is to prevent injury rather than always to leave the gymnast standing up.

c. The spotter must know exactly what movement the gymnast is attempting.

d. A gymnast with empathy for the spotter's role will communicate with her spotters.

2. Know how much spotting is expected and needed by the gymnast. If the spotter thinks the gymnast is ready to try the skill by herself, she should tell her so. The spotter who simply doesn't spot once to prove to the gymnast that she is ready to be on her own destroys all trust previously established. The gymnast who has been the victim of this tactic is often heard to say, "Promise to spot me?" This is a symptom of trust shattered by a previous spotter.

How do you wean a gymnast of a spot? If a gymnast is in fact ready to be on her own, tell her so. Then tell her that only a light spot will be provided on the next attempt. If the gymnast continues to find success with a light spot, the spotter should then tell her she will not spot at all on the next attempt. Of course, both spotter and gymnast should be aware that often the first attempt without a spot is poorer than the previous attempts. The spotter should take this into account as she determines when the gymnast is ready to move from a light spot to no spot at all.

3. Understand how to spot the movement being attempted. Effective spotting techniques can only be determined after a consideration of the mechanics involved in the movement itself.

Among the questions that should be considered as you determine the most effective spotting techiques to use are:

a. What are the mechanical principles involved? For instance, is there forward–backward rotation involved? Is motion involved that fights gravity?

b. What does the gymnast need from the spotter in order to complete enough of the skill to avoid injury? For instance, does the gymnast need more lift, momentum, a secure grip, balance, or speed?

c. How can the gymnast's needs be met most effectively? For instance, is more than one spotter needed, or is there a specific point where great stress on the grip occurs so that additional support might be needed? Is a spotting belt indicated?

4. Be physically able to provide an effective spot. If the spot for a particular movement requires a great deal of strength, arrange for a second spotter. If a taller spotter is needed, find one.

5. Be ready to spot at the same time the gymnast attempts the skill. Develop a discipline among your gymnasts so that they always make sure their spotter is ready before attempting the movement.

SPOTTING BELTS

A spotting belt provides: (1) a secure grip on the gymnast; (2) an easy way to provide lift at the correct moment; (3) an effective method of producing a soft, safe landing for an out-of-conrol gymnast; and (4) a good means of being in the right place at the right time in movements that involve running.

There are two types of belts and three types of suspensions. Types of belts are: (1) *regular* (used for most movements) and (2) *twisting* (used only for movements involving twisting).

Types of suspensions are: (1) *hand-held spotting belt* (2 persons—Figure 6-1), (2) *overhead suspension* (1 person), and (3) *overhead traveling suspension* (1 person).

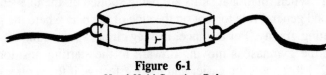

Figure 6-1
Hand-Held Spotting Belt

Whenever the belt is used, it should be snugly and securely fastened around the gymnast, with the attachments located on each side. The loose end of the belt beyond the buckle should be tucked away.

A hand-held spotting belt is often very helpful in spotting forward–backward rotational skills, such as front and back handsprings. Each of the two spotters should hold the rope tightly in one hand, close to the attachment to the belt. The spotter must *not* put a finger or thumb through the attachment ring.

The other hand should hold the loosely coiled remainder of the rope. The rope should *not* be wrapped tightly around the spotter's hand. The lifting and supporting is executed by the hand closest to the belt. If rotation is also needed, the loosely coiled rope can also be held by the hand closest to the belt while the now-free hand can assist in providing rotation.

The overhead suspension requires only one spotter and is particularly effective for advanced movements on the trampoline and beam. The rope should be held by two hands, one hand a foot or two above the other.

If the gymnast moves in preparation for the movement (for example, preliminary bounces for a front somersault on the trampoline) the spotter needs to allow the rope to move up and down with her hands as the gymnast moves. *There should never be any slack in the rope.*

The overhead traveling suspension is used in much the same way as the overhead suspension, except that the belt moves in a horizontal plane to accommodate the running gymnast. The spotter needs to move parallel to the gymnast, and, again, no slack should be permitted in the rope. The presence of slack in the rope results in a delay in the application of lift to the gymnast and, when the late lift is applied, it comes with a jolt. Thus slack in the rope can result in an ineffective spot and a hazardous attempt for the gymnast.

GENERAL TIPS ON SPOTTING

1. When rotational skills are being spotted on the uneven bars, it is a good general rule to spot on the side of the bars where the gymnast is fighting gravity. For instance, in a leg circle, spot behind the low bar where the gymnast is moving upward to the starting position.

2. Most spots are easier and more effective if the spotter contacts the gymnast near her center of gravity. This is particularly true of movements that require the spotter to provide lift.

3. The spotter should try to provide lift by using her leg muscles rather than depending on her back. Besides being healthier for the spotter, this provides a stronger spot when needed.

4. The use of the hand *plus* the forearm will provide a more reliable spot than the use of the hand only. The gymnast is less likely to slip away from the spotter's grip, and the spotter also will have greater lifting power.

5. The closer the spotter moves her own base of support to the gymnast, the easier it will be for her to spot. Care should be taken, though, to be sure that the spotter is not so close as to inhibit the body movements of the gymnast.

6. It is very difficult to catch up to a gymnast who is moving before the spotter is correctly positioned. Therefore, for appropriate movements, it is wise to have contact before motion is begun. In addition, preliminary contact gives more confidence to the gymnast, and it gives the spotter a better kinesthetic sense of what is happening during each phase of the skill. Often the spotter can analyze errors simply by feeling the rhythm of the movement.

7. Where the spot is used to provide balance or support, the spotter should consider using more of her body than just hands and forearms. For instance, when helping a gymnast to find the balance point in a handstand, the spotter can use her shoulder and knee to assist. Similarly, a forward roll on the balance beam can be balanced by the hip or side of the spotter, thus freeing the spotter's hands to assist other requirements of the skill.

There is more to spotting than just standing nearby. The challenge comes in training ourselves and our gymnasts in how to be effective spotters.

7

Tumbling and floor exercise

Floor exercise is an aesthetic melding of dance (and modern gymnastics movements) and tumbling performed to music within an area of about forty feet by forty feet. It is, in the minds of most people, the most expressive event in women's gymnastics. For this reason it is also the event where the "tennis shoe–leotard syndrome" is most pronounced. The tennis shoe–leotard syndrome refers to a beginner's embarrassment or uneasiness at trying to be graceful. Often the student who arrives at gymnastics from a background of team sports is the most likely candidate for an extreme case of the syndrome. Such a student's typical lack of flexibility adds to the problem. These students often make an unconscious determination that they are athletes (tennis shoe) and cannot be successful at "dancy, graceful" activities such as gymnastics (leotard). So they segregate themselves from anyone who shows gymnastics skill. They try a movement once, fail, and do not try again. They generally endure but do not enjoy their gymnastics experience.

As a teacher or coach, you are aware that movement is still movement regardless of whether it is a stretch at first base, a lunge in fencing, or an arabesque in gymnastics. It is an important challenge for you to get your students to understand this universality of movement. Floor exercise and tumbling offer the ultimate event for the challenge.

The use of compulsory rather than optional routines is a help. Having music playing during practice time seems to bring out the expressiveness in all your students, and somehow your tennis-shoe gymnasts' embarrassment and reticence are diminished under the cover of music.

The movements in this chapter are categorized (and presented progressively within each category) as forward rolls, backward rolls, inverted movements involving a handstand, and inverted movements requiring back flexibility. Movements requiring back flexibility have been segregated from the inverted movement category because back (and shoulder) flexibilty is often difficult and sometime requires more work and time to develop than is available in a class.

GROUND RULES

Mats

1. Select mats that do not bottom out and that provide *ample room* for the skill being practiced *plus room for errors*.

2. If using more than one mat in a row, *securely connect the mats* with velcro, tie the handles together, or use some other appropriate method of connecting them.

3. Use 4-inch thick landing mats, if available, for more difficult tumbling or when a performer is attempting a movement alone for the first few times.

4. Clean and disinfect the mats regularly. If a carpet covering is used, shampoo and vacuum it regularly.

Traffic Pattern

One-way traffic should become the rule in your gymansium. That is, rolls, cartwheels, handstands, and the like should be performed in one direction only.

FORWARD ROLLS

Forward Tuck Roll

Start

Squat with feet and knees together and hands shoulder width apart at least 2 feet in front of the feet, with fingers pointing in the direction of the roll.

Procedure

1. Lift hips by starting to straighten knees; tuck head to chest.
2. Use arms to gently lower the back of the head (not top) and then shoulders to the mat.
3. Leave the feet on the mat as long as possible so that, for a moment, the knees are straight.
4. Reach forward with arms as soon as shoulders begin to lift from the floor.
5. Shift weight foward onto feet to arrive at the starting position without using hands to get up.
6. Stand up with perfect balance (Figure 7-1, p. 74).

For the few students who need help in developing the proper movement pattern of the roll, an effective teaching spot is produced by standing to the side and a bit in front of the gymnast and grasping her hips on either side as she rolls. Her roll can thus be slowed down, the landing made softer, or the direction established.

Common Errors

1. Lifting one foot off the floor before the other. *Correction*: This error causes a heavier landing because it causes the back to flatten. This error is one for which there is a "miracle" and instant cure. Have your gymnast place a rolled-up sock or gymnastics slipper between her ankles and keep it there throughout the roll.
2. Placing the hands too close to the feet at the start of the roll. *Correction*: Reach farther in front. The symptoms of this error include a hard landing on the head or back.
3. Crossing the feet to get up at the end of the roll. *Correction*: Use a rolled-up sock held between the ankles as in the correction for error 1 above.
4. Inability to get up onto the feet at the end of the roll. *Correction*: There are several typical causes for this error, such as opening up from the tuck position too soon, allowing the back to relax and flatten out during the roll and thus decreasing the momentum, and failing to pull the feet close to the hips. Remember that a beginner may get easily frustrated by practicing the roll over and over. You can have her practice only the ending by simply rolling backward to the shoulders and then rolling forward.

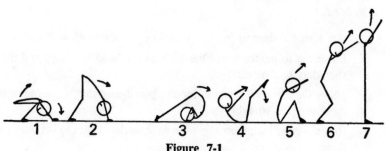

Figure 7-1
Forward Tuck Roll

Variations

Half-Straddle Forward Roll

Start: Straddle the legs as far as is comfortable. Pike and place hands on the floor facing the direction of the roll and about 2½ or 3 feet in front of feet.

Procedure: Tuck head toward chest; bend elbows as more weight is placed on the hands. Gently place back of head on mat and roll. As soon as the midback is on the mat, quickly tuck the legs and finish as for a tuck foward roll (Figure 7-2).

Common errors:

1. Placing the hands too close to the feet (symptom: hard landing).
2. Pushing off with feet instead of rolling weight off the feet.
3. Bending knees and failing to point the toes.

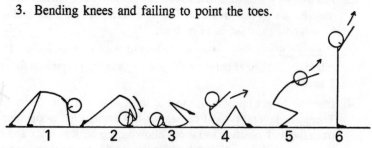

Figure 7-2
Half-Straddle Forward Roll

Forward Tuck Roll to a Pose

Some beginning gymnasts find it difficult to return to a standing position after a forward roll without using their hands to push themselves up. The forward roll to a pose provides these gymnasts with an easy, good-looking method for getting up from a forward roll until they perfect the transfer of weight necessary for getting up in the conventional manner. It is also useful as a variation in a routine.

Start: Begin as though performing a forward tuck roll or half straddle roll or front scale forward roll.

Procedure: When the lower back comes in contact with the mat, sharply bend the right knee and laterally rotate the leg at the hip so that the right foot is close to the left hip and the right knee is pointing off to the right side. Put the entire lower right leg on the floor as the roll continues. Reach forward with the left leg and place the left foot on the floor about two feet in front of the right leg. Allow the left knee to bend as it needs. Shift the weight forward so that the hips rise over the right leg and the roll is completed in a pose position (Figure 7-3).

Common error: Failing to put the entire side of the lower leg on the floor while starting the pose (symptom: difficulty getting up because the center of gravity is higher).

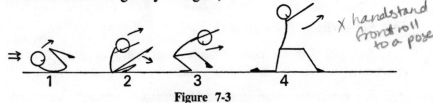

Figure 7-3
Forward Roll to a Pose

Front Scale Forward Roll (Arabesque)

Start: Assume a good arabesque or front scale position, with the left leg extended.

Procedure: Bend the supporting left knee slightly and reach toward the floor. Place the hands about 2 feet in front of the left foot in the same position as for other forward rolls. Bend elbows, tuck head, and continue as with a regular forward roll. The extended right leg remains extended until the roll has progressed to the back. Then both legs join, with the body piked. Immediately tuck and complete as a regular forward tuck roll or into a pose as described above (Figure 7-4).

Common errors:

1. Bending both legs at the start of the roll.
2. Bringing legs together late or failing to pike as legs come together.

Spotting: A spot is only needed if the gymnast needs help in finding the correct time to bring feet together, pike, and so on. Stand directly behind the gymnast, a little to the side of the supporting left leg. Place your left hand around her waist and your right hand on the outside of her thigh as she lifts her right leg into a front scale position. As she performs the forward roll, you can slow her down or stop her at any point and give her cues concerning piking, legs together, and the like. As her back contacts the mats, slide your hands down to her ankles and bring her ankles together.

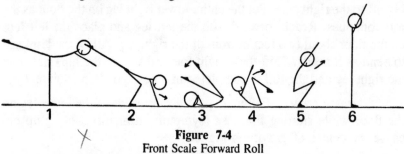

Figure 7-4
Front Scale Forward Roll

Full-Straddle Forward Roll

This roll is much more difficult to do than it appears. It is not dangerous, but rather takes timing and a good use of momentum.

Prerequisites: Half-straddle forward roll, warm-up with hamstring and adductor flexibility exercises.

Start: Same as for half-straddle forward roll.

Procedure: Same as for half-straddle forward roll, except as the back contacts the mat, keep the legs in a straddle position. It is very important to keep the back rounded and the chin tucked throughout the roll. As the hips contact the mat, place both hands between the straddled legs as close as possible to the pelvis and push down on the mat. Keep the head tucked and back rounded and complete the roll in a straddle position with all the weight on the feet. The roll is *not* completed if the hands are taking most of the weight (Figure 7-5).

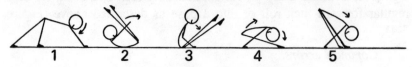

Figure 7-5
(Side View) Frontstraddle Roll

Common errors:

1. Placing the hands outside the legs to get up.
2. Bending the knees to get up.
3. Failing to place the hands as close as possible to the pelvis as the roll is being completed.
4. Allowing the back to flatten during the roll.

Verbal cues:

1. "Chin on chest."
2. "Go for second roll."
3. "Push down."

Combination: Forward straddle roll to half forward straddle roll.

BACKWARD ROLLS

In general, backward rolls are harder to master than forward rolls. This is due in part to the mechanical requirement of moving the center of gravity up and over the head. This is also the reason that the main common error is the inability to get over the head. (Sometimes a gymnast completes the roll but has taken a detour around the head and has instead performed a back shoulder roll.) There are two secrets for getting over the head in a backward roll:

1. More momentum.
2. More push with the hands as the gymnast is going over the head.

These techniques apply to all backward rolls.

Backward Tuck Roll

Start: Squat with feet together.

Procedure: Move backward so that hips contact mat but remain in a ball. Continue rolling backward. As the middle back contacts the mat, place the hands on the mat by the ears (palms toward mat, thumbs toward ears). Push against the mat with the hands and continue rolling in a ball. Place feet on the mat close to the hands, shift body weight backward onto the feet, and lower hips onto heels. Arrive at a balanced squat position and stand up (Figure 7-6).

Spotting: Stand to the side of the gymnast and about 2–3 feet behind her starting position. As soon as her feet leave the floor, reach over the rising feet and lift her at the hips. *Do not push.* This is a tricky spot because the spotter has very little time between the passing of the feet (position 4 in Figure 7-6) and the needed lift. Some spotters find it helpful to gently place the hand closest to the gymnast on her back before she begins the movement and then switch to the hips at the appropriate time. Placing the hand on the back gives the spotter a kinesthetic awareness of the gymnast's timing and helps the spotter know when to reach for the hips.

Common errors:

1. Rolling over the shoulder, allowing one forearm to touch the mat. *Correction:* "Roll straight over your head," or "keep the forearm off the floor."
2. Placing the hands with the little fingers closest to the ears (destroys the ability to push over the head).
3. Allowing the back to flatten out as it comes in contact with the mat (loss of momentum).
4. Failing to remain tightly tucked during the roll.

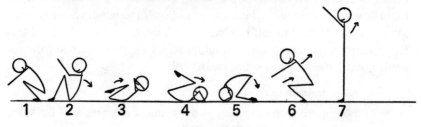

Figure 7-6
Backward Tuck Roll

Variations

Back Roll to a Straddle

Start: Same as for back tuck roll.

Procedure: When the shoulders contact the mat, straddle the legs out to the sides. The hand position and push is the same as for the back tuck roll. Keep toes pointed until just before they contact the mat. Finish in a straddle position (Figure 7-7).

Spotting: Spotting is difficult to accomplish because of the straddled legs, so if a safety spot is needed, have the gymnast perfect the spottable back tuck roll first.

Common errors: Some gymnasts find it easier to get over their heads with the straddle roll than with the tuck roll. Therefore, the error of a shoulder roll is less likely.

1. Bending knees.
2. Dorsal flexing the feet throughout the roll instead of properly keeping them pointed until just before they contact the mat.

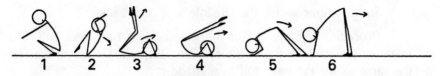

Figure 7-7
Half-Straddle Back Roll

Straddle to a Tuck Back Roll

Start: In a straddle position similar to the forward half straddle roll.

Procedure: Increase the pike while forcing the hips backward. Keep the chest close to the thighs as the hips drop backward and downward toward the mat. Reach between legs toward a spot about 1–2 feet behind feet on the mat. Hands touch the mat a moment before the hips do. As soon as the hips contact the mat, tuck the legs and complete the roll the same as for a back tuck roll (Figure 7-8).

Spotting: Because of the straddle, it is not feasible to spot this roll.

Common errors:

1. Placing the hands on the mat before the body weight is shifted backward. Instinct causes the gymnast to put her hands down early, but it prevents the gymnast from softening her landing. It may be helpful to point to a spot behind the gymnast as a target for her hands.
2. Failing to keep the chest close to the thighs.

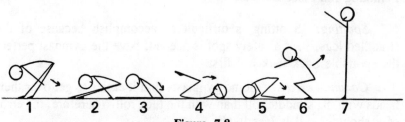

Figure 7-8
Straddle to Tuck Back Roll

Full-Straddle Back Roll

This roll begins and ends in a straddle and thus is really a combination of the two half-straddle rolls discussed above.

Start: Same as for the straddle to a tuck back roll.

Procedure: Same as for the straddle to a tuck back roll, but maintain the straddle position throughout the roll. Complete the roll the same as for the back roll to a straddle.

Note: Maintaining a straddle position throughout the roll is difficult for some gymnasts and requires strong hip flexors. It is quite acceptable to perform the roll with a momentary tuck as soon as the hips contact the mat, followed by another straddle as soon as the shoulders contact the mat. This tuck variation is much easier.

Spotting: As with all the straddle rolls, spotting is not possible.

Pose Variations

A back roll can be started in either a tuck or a straddle and yet end in a variety of poses, such as a knee scale, swan, or wolf (Figure 7-9).

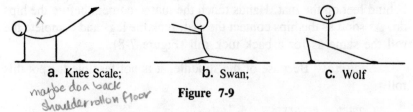

a. Knee Scale;   **b.** Swan;   **c.** Wolf

maybe do a back shoulder roll on floor

Figure 7-9

INVERTED MOVEMENTS

Two elements often pose problems for beginners learning inverted movements:

1. Ability to support the body weight on the hands.
2. Kinesthetic awareness of an inverted vertical position.

There are several lead-up activities that help the beginner overcome these problems. Lead-ups, such as the tip-up, tripod, chest stand, and shoulder stand, are found in Chapter 5. Other lead-ups for inverted movements involving the use of equipment (inverted hang on the stall bars and still rings) are found in Chapter 4.

Conditioning

Two areas on which beginners usually need to work before learning inverted movements are shoulder flexibility and elbow extension strength. Insufficient shoulder flexibility usually forces the gymnast to perform an inverted movement with excessive arch in the back. An excessive arch makes it difficult for the beginner to attain a vertical position. Elbow extension strength is needed in order to support the body weight.

Handstand

The handstand is a prerequisite to all other inverted movements. A gymnast can use either of two starting positions: a stride squat, or a standing start. Start 1 (stride squat; Figure 7-10) is best for a beginner's first few attempts. It is more difficult for her to kick up far enough to

Figure 7-10
Stride Squat Starting Position for Handstand

attain the vertical position, but this start affords her spotters a very secure spotting grip in case she bends her elbows or tucks her head (characteristic errors for the first few attempts). Start 2 (Figure 7-11) is a conventional start that, although it starts from a stand, passes through the stride squat position momentarily. As soon as your gymnast has shown you that she will not bend her elbows or tuck her head, have her switch from Start 1 to Start 2. The spotters must work harder with Start 2, but the gymnast has learned to avoid the typical common errors by practicing Start 1 first.

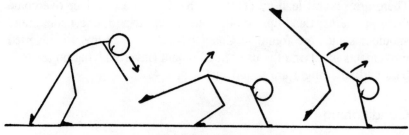

Figure 7-11
Standing Starting Position for Handstand

Procedure: Keep elbows totally extended. Focus eyes on a spot between hands.

Note: A helpful teaching device is to place a chalk mark for each hand and one in between for eye focus on the mat.

Kick left leg upward and over the base of support (hands) while pushing off the mat with the right leg. Elevate the hips up and over the base of support rather than allowing back to arch to absorb momentum of the kick. Stretch body toward ceiling and join legs overhead.

Note: Some gymnasts support their weight on arms with elbows pointing laterally. This position requires more effort than rotating the elbow (point of elbow/olecranon process) toward the starting position of the feet. So if your gymnast complains of feeling that her elbows are going to collapse, you might take a look at which direction her elbows are pointing. If they are pointing laterally, have her kneel on the mat with her hands in a handstand position. Then ask her to rotate her elbows. (This will not work unless the hands are immobilized by being on the mat.) Once she understands the correct position of the elbows, have her attempt the handstand again.

Note: There should be no more arch in the back than in good standing posture. Inflexible shoulders are often the cause of excessive arch.

Spotting:

For Start 1: Use two spotters, one on either side of the gymnast's shoulders. Spotter 1, at the gymnast's left shoulder, places her left hand around the gymnast's left shoulder to support the shoulder if the elbows are bent. The spotter's right hand is placed on the front of the left thigh to help lift the gymnast to a vertical position. Spotter 2 places her right arm across the gymnast's lower back and grasps the left hip. Her right hand is placed on the front of the right thigh to help the gymnast attain a vertical position (Figure 7-12).

It is the spotters' job to help the gymnast "feel" the vertical handstand position. It is also their job to prevent the gymnast from overbalancing. A competent spotting team will not allow the gymnast to overbalance and fall.

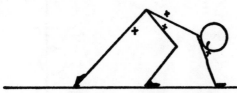

Figure 7-12
Spotting for Beginner's Handstand (spot at x's)

For Start 2: Use either one strong spotter or two spotters. As the gymnast kicks up and weight is being placed on her hands, each spotter (if two are used) reaches across the gymnast's lower back and grasps the opposite hip. The free hand is placed on the front of the closest thigh. Besides giving the gymnast the feel of the handstand and protecting against overbalancing, the spotters can lift the inverted gymnast a bit so that she can remove any excess arch in her back and concentrate on a total body extension before all of her weight is returned to her arms.

The spotters for both starts should maintain control until the gymnast has arrived at the starting position.

Common errors:

1. Bending the elbows.
2. Tucking the head toward the chest.

Note: In days gone by, there was a period when some gymnasts believed that a handstand performed with the head somewhat tucked (sometimes called a German handstand) was preferred form. This is not true today (Figure 7-13).

3. Arching the back (often caused by inflexible shoulders) (Figure 7-14).
4. Completing the handstand by bringing both legs down at the same time. This results in a heavy and fast landing.
5. Walking with the hands.

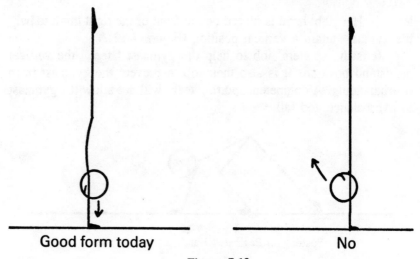

Figure 7-13
Handstand Form

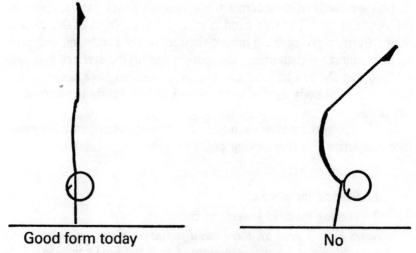

Figure 7-14
Handstand Form

Verbal cues:

1. "Stretch to the ceiling."

2. "Contract the abdominals." (This helps if the gymnast is arching too much.)

3. "Look at your thumbs." (Phrases such as "Tuck the head" lose their spatial orientation when the gymnast is inverted, so use cues that relate to an object or specific point.)

Precautions:

1. The spotters are not doing their jobs if a gymnast working on a handstand overbalances and falls to the mat. However, it is prudent to allow enough space and mat for this contingency.

2. Practicing handstands against a wall is ill-advised for gymnasts who have not perfected the handstand. First, if the gymnast happens to bend her elbows or tuck her head, she is likely to be injured. Second, most gymnasts kick up to the wall and then push off slightly to reach a balanced inverted position. Almost invariably, this produces a very arched handstand. So if you are using the wall as a "spotter" for your gymnasts who have mastered the handstand, be sure to have them kick up to a balanced position (hands about 1½ feet away from the wall) without touching the wall. If they overbalance and touch the wall, insist that they come down and try again rather than pushing back into an arched handstand.

3. It may be unwise for a beginner to be graded on whether she can attain and maintain a good handstand for a period of time without a light balance spot. In women's gymnastics, most handstands are momentary and are generally used as a transition into another movement, such as a walkover, roundoff, or cartwheel. The time a beginner will need to spend to be able to balance a good handstand for 3 seconds might be better spent working on some of the movements that *use* the handstand as a component.

Handstand–Forward Roll   *do a helie, too.*

In addition to being a movement that teaches and demands control, the handstand–forward roll is a movement that increases the gymnast's safety. Once she has mastered a handstand with a light spot, she should develop a method of practicing the handstand by herself that protects her in case she overbalances. The handstand–forward roll is such a movement.

Start: Attain a good handstand.

Procedure: Bend the elbows slowly, lowering the inverted body toward the mat. Just before the head would contact the mat, tuck the head quickly toward the chest. Round the upper back (abduct the scapula—"shoulder blades apart") and begin a roll. As the back contacts the mat, the legs, still extended, should be brought over the face in a semipiked position. As the waist touches the mat, tuck the legs and complete the movement as though performing a forward tuck roll (Figure 7-15).

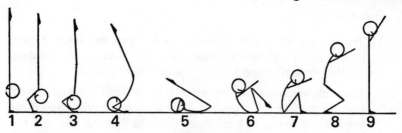

Figure 7-15
Handstand Forward Roll

Spotting: Use two spotters, one on either side of the gymnast's shoulders. Spot according to handstand-spotting technique. As soon as the gymnast has attained a good handstand position, shift both hands to the knee closest to the spotter and *slowly* let the gymnast down toward the mat. If using one spotter, grasp the gymnast around the hips and lower her to the floor.

After the gymnast has progressed to a skill level that requires very little spotting, have her try the handstand–forward roll on a 4-inch landing mat with a progressively lighter spot until all she needs is a balance spot for the initial handstand position.

Common errors:

1. Tucking the head prior to bending the arms. This produces a heavy landing. *Correction*: Start the learning progression for the handstand–forward roll with the class standing with arms overhead. Then, in a slow-motion repetitive drill, have the students look at their thumbs, make believe they are in a handstand, bend elbows, and finally, tuck the head and round the back (pulling elbows together in front of the face).

2. Piking as soon as the elbows start to bend. This results in a very heavy landing on the back. *Correction*: Correct this by spotting at the hips and not allowing the gymnast to proceed toward the mat if the hips start to pike.

3. Tucking the knees as soon as the elbows start to bend.

Variations:

1. Complete the roll in a pose.

2. Complete the roll in a straddle (as from a full-straddle forward roll).

Verbal cues:

1. "Elbows, *then* head."

2. "Melt into the mat, piece by piece—everything above the mat continues to do a handstand."

Cartwheel

The cartwheel is a very difficult movement because of its components: one-arm handstand, quarter turn, two-arm handstand, quarter turn, one-arm handstand. It is also a frustrating movement for most beginning gymnasts because, in its learning stages, the cartwheel feels very clumsy.

Prerequisite: Handstand with a balance spot.

Start: Standing with both feet on an imaginary line, right foot in front of left.

Procedure:

Step 1: Perform a crab by bending knees and torso sufficiently to place the right hand on the imaginary line about 2 feet in front of the right foot. Then place the left hand about a shoulder width farther along the line. Kick up the left leg slightly and swing it over to the line about 1–2 feet farther along than the left hand, followed by the right leg.

During the crab, concentrate on the correct hand and foot placement (Figure 7-16).

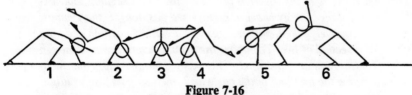

Figure 7-16
Crab (lead-up for cartwheel)

Step 2: Place increasingly more weight on the hands as the crab is performed. Lift the feet farther from the ground each time. Concentrate on finally having the left leg proceed directly over the head rather than out to the side. Soon the crab turns into a cartwheel with only form corrections needed.

The final cartwheel should be performed from a standing position facing the direction of the cartwheel and ending in a momentary standing position facing the direction from which the gymnast came, then a turn to a position parallel to the imaginary line. An even, four beat count should exist in the final cartwheel—hand, hand, foot, foot.

Spotting: The majority of spots needed in learning the cartwheel are to help the gymnast feel the correct movement rather than to ensure safety. One spotter is used. The spotter should stand to the side of the gymnast and a few feet in front of her starting position.

If the gymnast puts her right hand down first, the spotter must be on the right side of the gymnast. If the spotter mistakenly stands on the other side, the gymnast's feet are most likely going to kick the spotter. The spotter for a right-hand-first cartwheel should place her supinated left hand on the performer's right hip as the gymnast places her first hand on the mat. The spotter's right hand will be placed on the left hip as soon as the gymnast begins to be inverted. Thus, by grasping the gymnast's hips, the spotter can help balance, lift the hips over the base of support, slow the move, and so on.

Common errors:

1. Hands not on the imaginary line. This usually results in a less-than-vertical cartwheel.

Hint: Draw a chalk line on the mat and have your gymnast practice placing the hands and feet on the line as she attempts the cartwheel. This often results in a few off-balance cartwheels until she adjusts her body alignment, but there is no safety problem here.

2. Piking while in the inverted position.

Hint: Have your gymnast kick up for a cartwheel, but stop her when she is in the inverted position (just like a regular spot, except balance the gymnast in an inverted position). If the gymnast is excessively piked, pull her legs into a vertical position and hold for a second or two. Then have the gymnast come down as though from a regular handstand. This method allows the gymnast to practice the first half of the cartwheel, including its proper alignment, without having to be concerned with the second half.

3. Placing both hands on the mat at the same time.

4. Turning the hands laterally or putting weight only on fingers rather than on the palms too.

5. Sagging or arching the back as the body weight is inverted.

6. Failing to land facing the direction from which the cartwheel started (symptoms: falling onto pelvis). *Correction*: Spot in the regular position. Have the gymnast kick up into a handstand; spot for a balanced handstand; and then turn her hips a quarter turn as she separates her legs and completes the movement as though performing the last half of the cartwheel. This activity helps the gymnast feel the correct turn while not worrying about the execution of the first half of the cartwheel.

Variations

Cartwheel with an Approach

The use of a run and a hurdle to gain momentum that can be converted into height is found in many of the more advanced tumbling movements.

Procedure: Step left, step right, hop on left foot with right leg held in the air. Land from hop onto left foot, step on right, and perform cartwheel with right hand on mat first.

Verbal cues: "Step left, right, hop, step, cartwheel"

Note: The term hurdle *relates to the hop. After the gymnast masters the mechanics of the approach, have her perform an approach cartwheel with more speed and thus more momentum. An approach cartwheel is the first step in the progression to learning a one-arm cartwheel and an aerial cartwheel (no hands on mat).*

✗ One-Arm Cartwheel

Prerequisite: Approach cartwheel.

Procedure: Perform an approach cartwheel with moderate speed. Place the first hand down on the mat as usual, but keep the second hand slightly off the mat. As the cartwheel is perfected, increase the momentum.

Spotting: One spotter stands in the same position as that used for a regular cartwheel. It is wise for the spotter and gymnast to practice a few times together with a two-arm approach cartwheel so that the spotter can identify the location where the gymnast will be inverted. If the gymnast is performing a right-handed cartwheel, place both hands on her right hip as she performs the hurdle. Lift lightly as the gymnast begins to reach for the mat. This is an easy spot and yet is very effective. It is also the spot used for the aerial cartwheel.

Aerial Cartwheel

Prerequisite: One-arm cartwheel with an approach.

Procedure: Perform a one-arm approach cartwheel with progressively increasing momentum from the hurdle. Try to place less and less weight on the hand touching the mat. Finally, keep both hands close to but away from the mat. If needed, the hand can always be placed on the mat.

Some helpful points to concentrate on are:

1. Try to keep the chest up and away from the mat as the legs are kicking up and over.
2. During the last step (step following the hurdle) keep the knee behind the foot (Figure 7–17). This is called blocking.
3. Try to increase the speed with which the legs move up and over the head. A verbal cue that is often helpful is, "Have the second leg catch up with the first."

Spotting: Same as for one-arm cartwheel.

Precautions: If you are using strip mats rather than a floor exercise mat for the aerial cartwheel or any other movement that involves an approach, be sure that the strip mats will not separate.

The aerial cartwheel is not a particularly high-risk movement. Neither is it a movement that the majority of students will master in a class setting. However, the progression to learning the aerial cartwheel is a continuous one from the crab through the aerial cartwheel. Thus there is no reason why students cannot start and proceed as far as their interest and skill allow on the progression toward the aerial cartwheel.

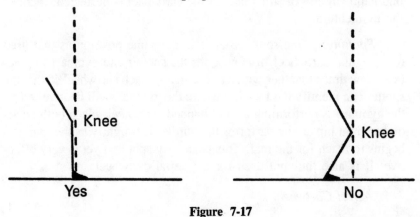

Figure 7-17
Blocking

Round-off

The round-off converts forward momentum into backward momentum.

Prerequisite: Cartwheel.

Start: Same as for cartwheel.

Procedure: Place the hands on the mat as though for a cartwheel or have the second hand down point toward the first. Kick the legs up and over the base of support in the same manner as for the cartwheel. The similarity to the cartwheel ends when the legs arrive at vertical. From this point on, the legs are brought together and the body makes a quarter turn while inverted. Then bring both legs down to the mat and land facing the direction from which the round-off was begun.

After mastering the round-off from a standing start, add an approach with a hurdle as though performing an approach cartwheel (Figure 7–18).

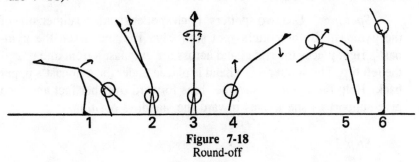

Figure 7-18
Round-off

INVERTED MOVEMENTS REQUIRING BACK FLEXIBILITY

Conditioning is particularly important for these movements. See Chapter 3 for suggestions on activities to increase back, upper back, and shoulder flexibility. It is also important to remember that not all gymnasts have, or can easily obtain, sufficient flexibility for these movements. Therefore it may be unwise to require all students to succeed with them.

Front Limber ✕ down to splits

Prerequisite: Handstand and a bridge.

Step 1

Start: Same as for a handstand.

Procedure: Perform a handstand. Without changing head or shoulder position, arch the back and start to bring the feet toward the mat. As the feet approach the mat they may be slightly separated. Land in a bridge (Figure 7–19, positions 1–4).

Step 2

In Step 1 the gymnast has practiced the first half of the movement. Step 2 allows her to practice the second half.

Start: From a supine position on the mat, push up into a bridge.

Procedure: Shift body weight forward over the feet. Extend knees and roll up piece by piece as though rolling hips, torso, and chin against a wall (Figure 7–19, positions 4–7).

Spotting: Use two spotters. Each spotter stands on either side of the gymnast. Both spotters spot similarly. The spotter on the gymnast's right places the right hand across the gymnast's front and grasps the left hip. The spotter's left hand is placed under the gymnast's upper back. Help the gymnast shift her hips forward over her feet and then give support as she moves toward the standing position.

Step 3

Now that the gymnast has practiced the first and second halves separately, it is time to put them together in the form of a complete limber.

Start: Same as for handstand.

Procedure: From the handstand, arch back and bring feet toward the mat. As soon as the feet contact the mat, shift the hips forward over the feet, extend the knees, and roll up to a stand. The head should be kept back, away from the chest, until a balanced stand is attained. Similarly, the hands should be overhead until a balanced stand is attained (Figure 7–19, position 7).

Spotting: Spot for the handstand in the regular way. As the gymnast begins to arch into the bridge, each of two spotters (one on either side of the gymnast) places her hands and forearms across the gymnast's upper back and hips to gently lower the gymnast into a bridge position. As soon as the feet touch the mats, with the hands and forearms still in place, the spotters gently help the gymnast shift her weight forward over her feet and then help lift the torso upward.

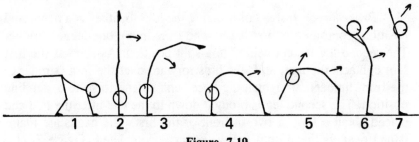

Figure 7-19
Front Limber

Common errors:

1. Allowing the shoulders to shift forward into an overbalanced position before the body has approached the bridge position (Figure 7–20).

2. Tucking the head toward the chest.

3. Failing to shift the hips forward over the feet as soon as the feet contact the mat in the bridge position.

4. Bringing the arms forward as the gymnast returns to a stand from the bridge.

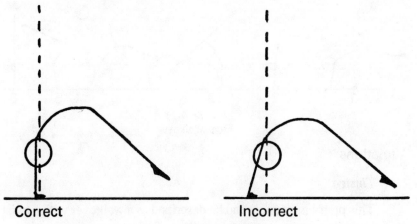

Correct   Incorrect

Figure 7-20
Shoulder Alignment

Front Walkover

Prerequisite: Front limber.

Conditioning: Back and shoulder flexibility.

Start: Same as for front limber, except that the legs should not be brought together in a handstand position.

Procedure: Instead of bringing the legs together in a handstand position, continue the first leg up and over into a one-legged bridge. The second leg is kept behind in a split position. As soon as the first foot contacts the mat, shift the hips forward over the foot (similar to the front limber), straighten the knee, and extend torso to a standing position. The second leg is brought down to the mat after the first and placed about a foot or two in front of the first. The hands are maintained over the head until the walkover is completed (Figure 7–21).

Spotting: Use two spotters, one on each side of the gymnast as she is in the inverted position. Some spotters find it more comfortable and effective to kneel rather than stand. Both spotters spot similarly. The spotter on the gymnast's right side places her inverted left hand on the inverted gymnast's upper right arm. The spotter's right hand is placed on the gymnast's upper back.

Note: For gymnasts who require a heavier spot, place the left hand on the upper back and the right hand on the hips.

Common errors: Same as for front limber.

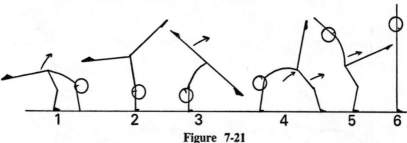

Figure 7-21
Front Walkover

Variations

Tinsica

This pretty movement can be described as a walkover with a twist in the middle or as a cartwheel walkout. Teach the tinsica just like a walkover, with the following exceptions: Place the right hand down first (assuming the gymnast is doing a right-hand tinsica), with fingers pointing toward the direction of the movement (same as a right-hand cartwheel). The second hand is then placed about 1 ½ feet farther in front.

The gymnast proceeds as though doing a regular front walkover. As she approaches the final standing position, she should, however, turn her head slightly to look at the last hand remaining on the mat, in this case her left hand.

Spotting: Use the same spot as for the front walkover.

Common errors: Same as the walkover plus arriving in the final position off balance because of the twist in the torso.

Note: The twist is very slight and returns to the starting, straight-on torso position of a walkover at the completion of the movement.

Front Handspring

The front handspring does not require the same degree of flexibility as the walkover or tinsica. So once your gymnasts have mastered the hurdle found in the approach cartwheel, they are ready to try the handspring if they have a little back flexibility.

Start: Same as for approach cartwheel.

Procedure: Perform an approach and hurdle. Then place both hands on the mat at the same time as though performing a handstand. Kick the left leg upward at the same time. Follow by quickly kicking the right leg and try to have it catch up with the left by the time the left leg reaches vertical. At this point, the body alignment should be similar to a good handstand. Push the mat away with a thrust that is initiated from the shoulders. (Do not bend the elbows to push.) Arch the back slightly as the legs are moving quickly overhead to the mat. The landing position should be in a good standing posture with the arms extended overhead and the chin lifed up, away from the chest. (Figure 7–22).

Spotting: Same as for the front walkover.

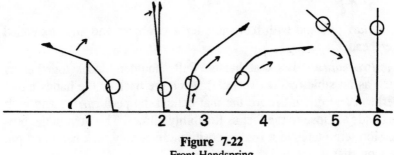

Figure 7-22
Front Handspring

Common errors: Same as for the front walkover, plus

1. Dropping the arms to the sides as soon as the hands leave the mat.
2. Failing to put a lot of speed in the kick of the legs. The legs must travel faster than for the walkover or tinsica.

Approach Walkover

Add an approach and hurdle prior to the walkover. This is also sometimes called a spring walkover.

Approach Tinsica

Add an approach and hurdle prior to the tinsica. This is also sometimes called a spring tinsica.

Note: All of the front walkover variations are quite similar mechanically. Thus when a gymnast begins to master one movement, she often can quickly master all the variations.

Back Walkover

Unlike the 'blind' front walkover, the back walkover and most other backward movements are "sighted." The gymnast performing a back walkover can see the mat and her landing target during at least the last two-thirds of the movement. This factor seems to make backward movements easier. However, most gymnasts find it scary to initiate a backward movement. So the spotter should be sure that the gymnast feels her contact with her before the movement starts.

Prerequisites: Handstand with a balancing spot, and a bridge.

Conditioning: Shoulder and back flexibility.

There are three steps in the progression for learning a back walkover. They are:

Step 1

Start: Stand with feet shoulder width apart and arms extended over head.

Procedure: Look at hands. Pull shoulder blades together as much as possible (adduct scapula). Arch the back as the hands move overhead and down toward the mat behind the performer. Land with the hands as close to the feet as flexibility allows. This step in the progression terminates in a bridge position, so simply tuck head and put back on mat.

Spotting: Use two spotters, one on either side of the standing gymnast. The spotter on the right side of the gymnast places her right arm across the front of the gymnast, and the hand is placed on the side and back of her left hip. The spotter's left hand is placed on the gymnast's upper back. The second spotter performs in a similar manner on the other side. Both spotters assist the gymnast by lowering her (very slowly at first) to the bridge position.

Common errors:

1. Failing to stretch at the start.
2. Failing to pull shoulder blades together.
3. Failing to look at hands throughout.

Step 2

Start: Stand with one foot slightly in front of the other, arms extended over head. Both legs should be slightly laterally rotated from the hip (Figure 7-23, positions 1–3).

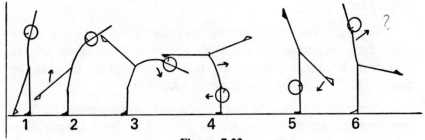

Figure 7-23
Back Walkover

Step 3

Complete back walkover.

Start: Same as for Step 2.

Procedure: Same as for Steps 1 and 2 until the hands are almost in contact with the mat. At this point forcefully lift the forward leg up and over the body, followed by the other leg. Maintain a split position of the legs. As the legs are kicked up and over, the hands contact the mat, and the torso and arms must be ready to support the body in an inverted, split-legged handstand position as the legs pass over the center of gravity. The first leg kicked up is the first leg to land on the mat on the other side. Ideally, the second leg should be maintained above the mat while the body moves to a front scale/arabesque finish position. More realistically, the body ends in a standing position (Figure 7–23).

Spotting: Hands are placed on the upper back and the back of the thigh.

Hint: Transferring the body's center of gravity over the hands so that the walkover can be completed is often the trickiest part of the movement. Try to have your gymnast lift her head as much as possible when the hands contact the mat. Ask her to arch her back more or think of shifting her torso toward the landing site.

Common errors: Same as for Steps 1 and 2, plus:

1. Getting stuck in bridge position. This is usually caused by having the hands too far away from the feet or failing to shift the center of gravity over the hands.
2. Pushing one leg against the spotter's hand to enable the other leg to move over the head more easily.

Back Handspring

The back handspring (sometimes called a flip flop) is a movement that is inappropriate for use in a beginning class. However, in a club or on a team, it is one of the first of the more advanced movements that your gymnasts will need to know.

Procedure: Lock the body into a stiff, stable position. Lift the arms to a position directly over head and look at hands. Do not allow arms to pass beyond the vertical. If the body is locked, this simple motion of the arms will cause the body to begin to fall backward. Maintain the stiff, stable position. When the body has traveled backward to the angle shown in Figure 7–24, positions 1–3, quickly bend the knees slightly and then extend them so that a small jump is given upward at the same angle.

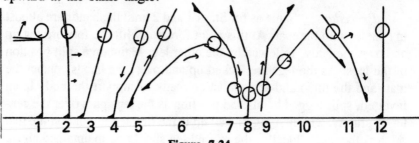

Figure 7-24
Back Handspring

With the aid of effective spotting, the gymnast will be projected into an inverted position (momentary handstand), from which she pushes with straight elbows so that a small amount of repulsion is created. She will then land on her feet (Figure 7–24).

Note: There are many, many ways of learning a back handspring. The method above is presented because it: (1) can be safely spotted by fellow students, (2) is unlikely to develop a handspring that is too arched (3) is unlikely to develop a handspring that undercuts itself (landing too close to take-off location). The starting point should be 3 feet to body length (for series) from hand contact.

Spotting: Use two spotters, one standing on each side of the gymnast, facing each other. The spotters join hands across the gymnast's upper back with the hand closest to the gymnast's back. The spotters join the other hands across the back of the gymnast's hips. As the gymnast jumps, help support her in a teeter-totter and "pour" the gymnast into a handstand position. This is a more secure spot than the typical back handspring spot, which involves just placing a hand on the back and thigh of the gymnast. A secure spot is vital to this movement because one of the common errors is the bending of the elbows by the gymnast, which results in her falling on her head.

Common errors:

1. Unlocking the hips and allowing the hips to move forward in a slight arch during the early stages of the handspring.

   Hint: To accentuate the need for locking the hips, stand behind the gymnast with your hands ready to catch her back when she moves 5–10 inches backward from vertical standing position. Have her move her arms from horizontal to vertical.

   If her hips are locked she will correctly move backward.

2. Bending the elbows when contacting mat.
3. Undercutting.

SOME BASIC DANCE MOVEMENTS

Most beginning gymnasts, who might also be suffering from a mild case of the tennis shoe-leotard syndrome, find leaps among the least intimidating of the dance movements.

Stride Leap

This leap, sometimes called a split leap, is in actuality a larger-than-usual running step. Because of this, it can be introduced by having your gymnasts run and leap over an imaginary barrier, such as a "3-foot wide river with alligators in it," and continue their run on the other side.

Procedure: Step left, lift the right leg up into the air in front of the body, and extend the left leg as it comes off the floor toward the rear. Land on the right leg (Figure 7–25).

Note: Don't forget to bend the right knee upon landing to help absorb the shock.

Common errors:

1. Bending the back (left) leg while in the air.
2. Failing to absorb the landing.

Spotting: Spotting is not needed for safety. However, many beginners find it easier to concentrate on the correct leg position if two spotters (one on each side) grasp the gymnast's lower arm and give her a little extra lift for a little extra time in the air.

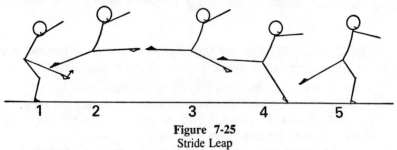

Figure 7-25
Stride Leap

Stag Leap

This is a variation of the stride leap. The forward leg is bent while the gymnast is in the air (Figure 7–26).

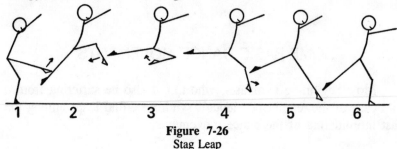

Figure 7-26
Stag Leap

Hitch Kick

This movement is sometimes called a scissors leap.

Procedure: Step left and lift right leg up into the air in front of the body. Lift the left leg up into the air in front of the body so that it passes the right as the right is on its way back down to the floor. Land on right leg, then left.

Verbal cue: "First leg up is first leg down."

Common errors:

1. Bending the knees or failing to extend the ankles.
2. Trying to cover too much ground. (The hitch kick is basically a stationary movement.)

Sitz Jump or Leap

Procedure: Step left and lift right leg up into the air in front of the body. Immediately and forcefully bend the left knee so that the left heel comes close to or in contact with the hips. Extend the left leg and land on it. Then bring the right leg down (Figure 7–27).

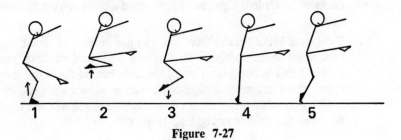

Figure 7-27
Sitz Jump

Cabriole

Conceptually, the cabriole and sitz jump are quite similar. In the cabriole, instead of bringing the left leg up to the hips, it is maintained in an extended position and brought in contact with the other leg.

Procedure: Step left, lift the right leg up into the air in front of the body (not too high). Immediately lift the left leg up to meet the right. Then bring the left leg back to the mat. Then the right leg returns to the mat (Figure 7–28).

Verbal cues: "First leg up is last leg down."

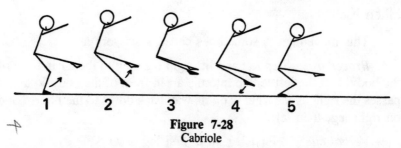

Figure 7-28
Cabriole

Floor exercise consists of tumbling and creatively adapted movements from dance and modern gymnastics. Selecting movements from the balance beam section, the leaps presented above, and variations of the body wave presented below will help you develop beginning routines that will provide your gymnasts with an opportunity to be exposed to floor exercise.

Body Wave

Start: Stand with arms at sides.

Procedure:

1. Contraction: Bend knees, contract abdomen, tuck head and turn backs of hands into hips and slightly bend elbows toward front of body.

2. Extension: Make believe there is a wall just in front of you. Bring your knees to the wall, then thighs, hips, abdomen, rib cage, and chin. As this is being done bring the arms behind the body, then extend them and make a large circle with arms backward and upward so that they arrive at an upward stretch position at the same time that the chin is brought up (Figure 7–29).

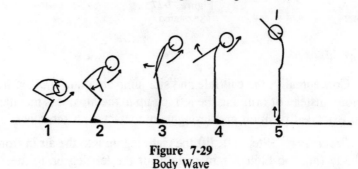

Figure 7-29
Body Wave

ROUTINES

When you are creating floor exercise routines, plan so that a large segment of your class can perform the routine simultaneously. A routine that takes a space of 30×10 feet, although it doesn't meet the official requirements of a 40×40-foot floor exercise routine area, does allow you and your gymnasts to work together.

Below are two sample routines for beginners. If music is available to you, use it in the construction of your routine. Besides more closely paralleling a real floor exercise routine, music gives the beginning gymnast timing cues and a sense of expressiveness which are difficult to create in any other manner.

Routine 1

1. Stand with weight on left foot, right foot extended behind, toe touching floor.
2. Step backward onto right foot.
3. Drag left foot close to right and perform a standing pivot turn to the right.
4. Run right, left; lift right leg into the air and perform a stag leap. (Land on right.)
5. Step left.
6. Standing pivot turn to a squat position.
7. Back roll to a straddle (half-straddle back roll).
8. Half-straddle forward roll.
9. Perform a body wave as you get up to a stand from the forward roll.
10. Cartwheel.
11. Half turn to original, starting pose (Figure 7–30).

Note: Routine 1 takes only forward and backward space. Therefore, a number of gymnasts can perform it at the same time with a need only for adequate safety space between them.

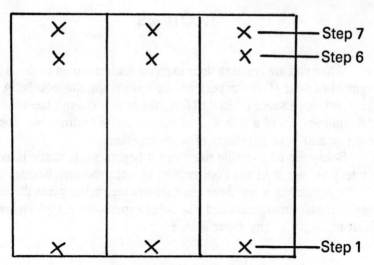

Figure 7-30
Three Gymnasts Performing Parallel Routines

Routine 2

1. Starting Pose: Kneel on left knee, hips extended, right leg straight out to the side with right foot on mat; right arm extended vertically, left arm extended horizontally to the left.

2. Sit on floor to the left of the left knee and rotate torso so that it turns one quarter to the right to face the right foot.

3. From this position perform a back tuck roll. Jump to a stand.

4. Step left and perform a hitch kick.

5. Step and perform a cartwheel to a body wave.

6. Perform a handstand forward roll directly from the body wave.

7. Complete the forward roll from the handstand in a pose.

8

Uneven parallel bars

There are two basic types of uneven parallel bars (Figures 8-1 and 8-2). Many schools prefer the free-standing bars for class instruction, but if you are planning on using the bars mainly for a team, you might select the cable bars instead.

Following is a list you may find useful in considering which type of bars to purchase.

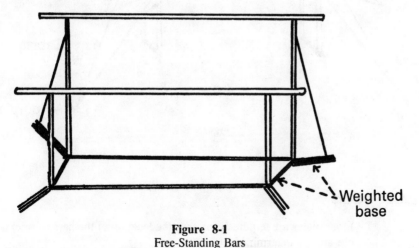

Weighted base

Figure 8-1
Free-Standing Bars

Free-Standing Bars

1. There are conversion kits that can be used to convert the men's even parallel bars into women's uneven parallel bars. For many schools the ability to have one set of bars serve two functions is a definite advantage.

2. The free-standing bars provide less stability for some of the advanced movements.

3. Height and width adjustments are easy to make, and the extent of those adjustments is adequate for beginners in most cases. However, for the unusual case requiring an extreme width adjustment, or for the more advanced gymnast, the cable bars are often the better choice.

4. Location is completely flexible since no floor plates are used.

5. Students find most brands of free-standing bars much quicker and easier to set up and take down than cable bars.

6. The presence of the base gives an uneven landing area beneath the bars.

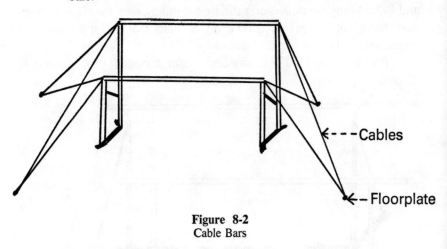

Figure 8-2
Cable Bars

Cable Bars

1. Floor plates are required, and thus the location of the bars is inflexible and predetermined.

2. Greater stability is provided for the advanced movements.

3. Transporting the bars to storage or to prepare them for use is difficult with most brands and requires some degree of supervision.

4. Cable bars are more flexible and provide more spring than the free-standing bars.

5. Extreme height and width adjustments are more available with cable bars.

6. The area underneath the bars is clear of obstruction, so the below-bar landing area is flat.

Equipment

Place a strip of mats at least 6 feet wide and 12 feet long underneath the bars. If you are working on dismounts, put more mats in the direction that the dismount takes the gymnast. Although you can safely place bars quite close together (side to side), you should provide at least 12 feet of open space in front of and behind the bars.

Sand the bars whenever they become rough from a build-up of chalk.

Hand Care

Using handguards helps retard the development of blisters. Handguards are generally of two types. Lampwick handguards are woven, heavy cloth. The second type is leather handguards, which are available in various designs. Whichever type you select for your gymnasts, make sure the gymnasts:

1. Break-in new handguards thoroughly by using them for simple movements before using them for circling or other movements where a firm grip is vital.
2. Work chalk into the handguards thoroughly; also put chalk on the hands underneath the handguards.

Blisters and calluses will develop to some extent with or without handguards. Smooth calluses are desirable; blisters and calluses with rough edges are not. Blisters and torn calluses are more likely to develop when the hands are hot from extended use.

Calluses should be rubbed with a pumice stone to keep them smooth. Hand lotion should be put on the hands as soon as practice or class is over. Chalk is very drying, and allowing it to remain on the hands increases the chance of roughness, which in turn increases the chance of torn calluses.

If a gymnast has a torn callus, do not let her work on the bars until it is entirely healed. The hand should be kept lubricated with cream or lotion until the new skin is no longer pink. If it is not lubricated, the new skin often will crack, and the healing process will take even longer.

Conditioning for the Bars

Plan your conditioning program for the bars around the following main areas:

1. Elbow extension strength.
2. Trunk flexion strength (abdominal strength).
3. Shoulder extension (extension of the arm at the shoulder).
4. Hip flexion strength.
5. Wrist and hand flexion strength.

Grips

Although beginners generally use only the three grips listed below, other grips, such as the eagle and crossed mixed grips, are used for more advanced movements.

1. Regular grip (also call an overhand or forward grip):   The hands are pronated. The grip is used for most support situations, such as the straight-arm support, and for most backward circling movements, such as the back hip pullover mount and the back hip circle (Figure 8-3).

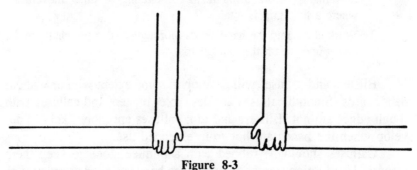

Figure 8-3
Regular Grip

2. Reverse grip (also called an underhand or backward grip): The hands are supinated. The grip is used for most forward circling movements, such as the leg circle (Figure 8-4).

3. Mixed grip: One hand is in a regular grip, and the other is in a reverse grip. This grip is used in such movements as the thigh roll (Figure 8-5).

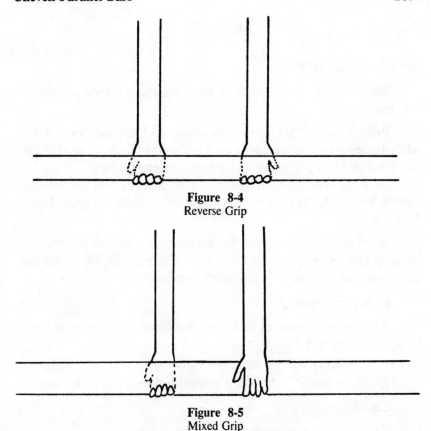

Figure 8-4
Reverse Grip

Figure 8-5
Mixed Grip

Encourage your gymnasts to grip the bar with their thumbs and fingers going in the same direction for circling movements. If your gymnasts feel secure enough, they can use the opposed thumb grip for stationary skills, such as straight-arm supports and shoot-throughs.

MOVEMENTS ON THE BARS

For convenience, movements on the uneven parallel bars are divided into the following four categories: mounts, circling movements, transitions (from one bar to the other or from one position to another), and dismounts. It is not necessary to master one category of movements before proceeding to the next. Rather, there is a progression of movements within each category. The simple movements are presented first within each category.

MOUNTS

Straight-Arm Support

Start: Stand facing the low bar (either side); forward grip on low bar.

Procedure: Quickly and forcefully pull the bar toward you while jumping up and forward as the bar springs back. Extend the elbows and end in a position with the hips between the hands on the low bar. The body should be straight or slightly arched, with the head up, elbows extended, legs together, and hands close to the hips (Figure 8-6).

Spotting: Stand behind the gymnast and, as she jumps, give some assistance by lifting her hips. Once she is on the bar, place one hand over her legs to keep her from overbalancing.

Common errors:

1. Standing too close to the bar and thus jumping straight up instead of forward and up.
2. Insufficient strength for elbow extension.
3. Piking instead of holding a straight body position on the bar.

Connections:

1. Forward roll dismount from low bar.
2. Swan balance.

Figure 8-6
Straight Arm Support

Back Hip Pullover Mount

Start: Stand facing the low bar (either side); forward grip on low bar.

Procedure: Shift weight to right foot and kick left leg up forcefully. At the same time bend the elbows and pull the bar toward waist and hips. Do not throw head back, but rather keep it in a neutral position. Lift the right leg and have it join the left as both legs move up and over the bar as though kicking over the head. The body should pike strongly as soon as the legs pass over the bar. "Thighs to face," "Knees to nose," and "Jackknife" are useful verbal cues. Extend the back toward a straight-arm support position, beginning with the lower back and ending with the head (Figure 8-7).

Spotting: If the gymnast's back is toward the high bar, two spotters should stand in front of the low bar and to the side of the performer. Place the arm closest to the low bar under the performer's lower back as soon as it can be reached. Place the arm farthest away from the bar on the underside of the gymnast's thigh as she kicks upward. Help lift the hips toward the bar and the legs up and over the bar.

Common errors:

1. Allowing elbows to straighten (symptom: hips dropping and shins hitting bar).
2. Kicking leg and hips forward rather than upward. (Even though it is counterintuitive, have gymnasts start closer to the bar.)
3. Stopping the backward rotation or getting stuck with legs over the bar. (Ask gymnast to accentuate the pike.)

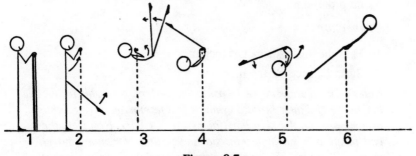

Figure 8-7
Back Hip Pullover Mount

Variations

Single-Leg Pullover

The single-leg pullover is a transition from the low to high bars rather than a mount. It offers the gymnast a chance to practice the hip lift and elbow contraction necessary for the back hip pullover mount.

Start: Hang from high bar with a regular grip and face the low bar. Place the ball of the left foot on the low bar, with knee bent. Rest the back of the right thigh on the low bar and extend the right leg.

Procedure: Bend the elbows and pull the waist and hips toward the high bar. As the hips approach the high bar, kick the right leg up and over the high bar, push off the low bar with the left leg, and have it join the right over the bar. Finish in the same manner as the back hip pullover mount. Cues such as "Hip up, then, kick," or "Hips—kick" may be helpful (Figure 8-8).

Spotting: Stand between the bars with your back to the low bar. Place your left hand on the gymnast's right hip and right hand on her left hip. Lift the hips. If the student does not kick or lift hips sufficiently high to finish the movement, help her bring her hips and feet down slowly to the low bar.

Common errors:

1. Kicking before the hips are lifted to a position about 6 inches from the high bar.
2. Allowing the elbows to straighten.
3. Throwing the head back. (This causes the back to arch and tends to drop the hips.)

Connections:

1. Skin the snake dismount (beginners).
2. Swan balance on the high bar.

Note: There are very few transition movements available for the beginning and intermediate gymnast that terminate in a straight-arm support on the high bar (facing the low bar). However, the end position is an important starting position for many movements. Therefore, the single-leg pullover, which is the easiest of these transition movements, should be taught very early in the gymnast's introduction to the uneven bars.

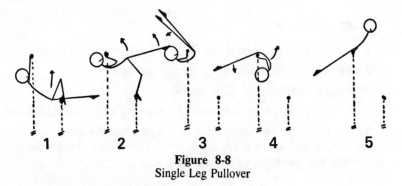

Figure 8-8
Single Leg Pullover

Long Hang (To Straddle or Pike over the Low Bar)

Start: Stand beneath the high bar, facing the low bar.

Procedure: Jump and catch the high bar in a regular grip and then:

1. Pike over the low bar: Pike slightly, then arch, then quickly pike strongly and place feet or backs of thighs on low bar. The secret is to have an uneven rhythm for the pike-arch-pike. The rhythm should be pike (swing forward), then arch (don't wait for swing backward), then immediately pike. So, pike---------arch-pike.
2. Straddle over the low bar. Use same uneven rhythm as for pike.

Thigh Roll

Start: Stand beneath the high bar, facing the low bar.

Procedure: Jump up and grasp the high bar in a mixed grip, with the right hand in a reverse grip and the left in a regular grip. Use the uneven rhythm described above for the long-hang-pike over mount, pike------arch-pike, and bring the right leg up and over the low bar so that the back of the thigh is resting on the bar. Lift the left leg sideward and upward between the bars. Continue the circular path, with the left leg across the body and downward between the bars on the other side as you roll to the right on the right thigh. The hands may and should change grip as frequently as the need is felt during the turning process. Allow the hips to shift over the low bar at the completion of the 180° turn so that you finish in a stride seat on the low bar, facing the high bar. The left leg will be forward of the body and the bar while the right leg will be behind the body and the bar. The body weight will be on the back of left thigh, and the body will be facing the high bar (Figure 8-9).

Common errors:

1. Getting confused about where the legs are supposed to go.
2. Failing to shift the weight over the low bar.
3. Failing to shift grip when needed.
4. Allowing the left leg to lower and join the right leg over the low bar.

Note: The thigh roll can be done from any long-hang position and need serve only as a mount—for instance, a forward roll over the high bar (back facing the low bar), half twist, thigh roll, leg circle.

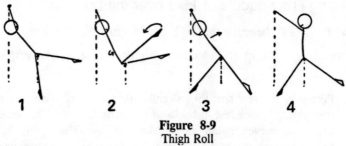

Figure 8-9
Thigh Roll

Glide Kip

This is a more advanced mount, so don't expect all students to master it. The mount is learned in two parts, glide and kip.

Glide

Start: Place hands on top of the low bar in a regular (forward) grip while standing about 1 foot behind the bar. Bend over and pike so that there is a straight line between hands and hips and another straight line between hips and feet (Figure 8-10).

Procedure: Maintain the pike position as the body swings forward in front of the bar. Make sure that the shoulders do not rise—there must be a straight line between hands and hips. If possible, maintain the swing until the starting position is regained.

Spotting: Two spotters kneel about 4–5 feet in front of the low bar and face each other. Each spotter reaches for the gliding gymnast's ankles with the hand that is farthest away from the bars. The ankle is then pulled outward, in front of the bar, and supported during the glide about 6 inches above the floor. The spotter's other hand reaches for the gymnast's lower back or hips and assists in providing forward and outward momentum. As the gymnast begins to glide back under the bar, release the hand on her back but assist the ankle as far as possible.

Common errors:

1. Failing to maintain a straight line between the hands and hips. (This will cause the "bend" to be released as the gymnast passes under the bar, and the changing position will cause the feet to drop to the floor.)
2. Bending the knees (usually due to lack of hip flexion strength).

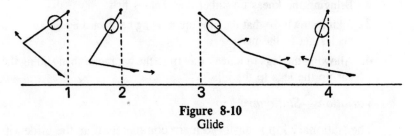

Figure 8-10
Glide

Kip

Start: The kip portion of the glide kip begins at the point of greatest forward swing from the glide.

Procedure: Sharply pike and bring the ankles up to the bar. Try to have the ankles up to the bar while the hips remain low and forward of the bar. The forward position of the hips is necessary for the proper kip action to be possible. As soon as the ankles arrive at the low bar, begin pulling the bar up the leg to the hip, with the arms straight. The force for the pulling action comes from the latissimus dorsi and other arm (at the shoulder) extensors. As the bar is being pulled toward the hips, gradually extend the legs backward. Finish in a straight-arm support (Figure 8-11).

Spotting: Same as for glide, except stand. You will have to bend over during the glide portion. As the gymnast begins the kip portion of the glide kip, help pike the legs to the bar while slightly

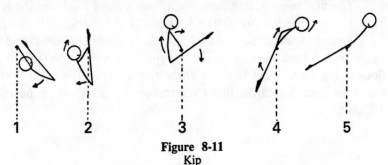

Figure 8-11
Kip

retarding the backward swing of the hips. As soon as the ankles approach the bar, help the gymnast pull her hips to the bar while allowing her legs to move backward.

Common errors:

1. Bending elbows (sometimes called "muscling up" in gymnastics jargon).
2. Bringing the knees up rather than ankles first.
3. Piking slowly so that the hips are moving backward by the time the ankles get to the bar.
4. Allowing the legs to move away from the bar rather than sliding the bar up the legs to the hips.

Variations—Stationary Kip

The stationary kip is easier to learn completely than the glide kip because it does not involve the glide portion of the glide kip.

Start: Grasp the high bar in a regular grip, facing the low bar. Place both legs over the low bar so that the upper back thighs or hips rest on the low bar.

Procedure: Keeping the elbows straight, arch the body so that the legs momentarily drop below the level of the low bar. Then forcefully pike and bring the ankles to the high bar while the hips stay as close as possible to the low bar. Then proceed in the same manner as described above for a glide kip.

CIRCLING MOVEMENTS

Most gymnasts find the circling movements to be the main source of fun on the uneven bars. They are indeed the core of good uneven bar work.

The first two circling movements you should teach are the back hip circle and the leg circle. The back hip circle resembles the feeling the gymnast experienced when learning the back hip pullover, and because it is a backward motion, the gymnast doesn't have to see the floor rising up to meet her. For these two reasons it is often best to teach the back hip circle first even though the leg circle is no more difficult.

General Principle for Spotting Most Circling Movements

Spot on the side of the bar where the gymnast is fighting gravity. For example, when your gymnast is performing a back hip circle on the low bar (back to high bar), you should spot in front of the bar. The gymnast is moving upward (fighting gravity) in front of the bar.

Back Hip Circle

Start: Start in a straight arm support position with regular grip on the low bar.

Cast

Procedure: Pike the legs under the bar while allowing the shoulders to move forward slightly to maintain balance. Forcefully extend hips and swing legs backward so that hips are pulled off the bar and the weight is supported momentarily on the hands. Maintain this body position as the body swings back toward the bar. Allow the body to pike slightly only when the hips contact the bar, not before.

Note: It is wise to break down the back hip circle into the cast (Figure 8-12, positions 1–4) and the following circle.

Spotting for cast only: Stand at the gymnast's side, between the bars. As she begins the leg lift portion of the cast, gently assist in the lift by placing the hands on the front part of her thighs.

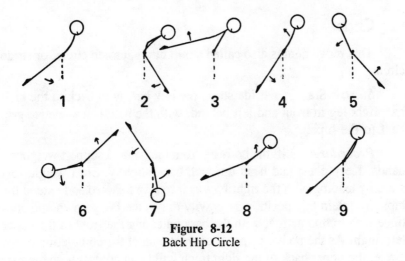

Figure 8-12
Back Hip Circle

Common errors:

1. Bending the elbows.
2. Throwing the head back.
3. Straddling legs or bending knees.
4. Piking before the hips return to the bar.

Back Hip Circle

Procedure: As the hips return to the bar after the cast, drop the shoulders back and down slightly and begin the circle. End in a straight-arm support. The elbows should remain straight, particularly at the end of the movement (Figure 8-12, positions 5–10).

Spotting: Same as for back hip pullover mount.

Common errors:

1. Throwing the head back.
2. Piking before the hips hit the bar (symptom: hips drop and body goes in front of bar instead of circling).
3. Dropping shoulders forward as hips contact the bar (symptom: the circling momentum is lost and the body drops below the bar).

Note: A gymnast learning the circle needs to pike. However, once the cast is perfected, a layout position should be sought.

Leg Circle

This movement is also called a mill circle, crotch circle, or stride circle.

Start: Start in a stride sit on the low bar, with back to the high bar, right leg in front and left behind, with the hands in a reverse grip next to the hips.

Procedure: Lift the body up from the bar and support weight on hands. Keep chest and head up; arch back slightly. Shift weight forward by leading with the right foot as if to step forward and extend the hips. Maintain this position as gravity draws the body down and continue the circling action, with the bar contacting the front of the upper left thigh. As the body begins its upward path at the completion of the circle, the upper back of the right thigh will be in contact with the bar.

If more upward momentum is needed to complete the circle, press down with the right thigh. Return to the starting position (Figure 8-13).

> *Hint: If the gymnast has trouble gathering enough momentum to return to the starting position, she can try pulling the right thigh up toward the chest (straight knee) just as the circle starts. If the gymnast has so much momentum at the end of the circle that a second circle is likely, she can absorb the extra momentum by separating the legs as far as possible in a stride position, arching the back, and lifting the head.*

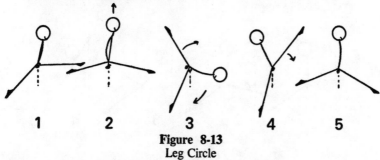

Figure 8-13
Leg Circle

Spotting: Two spotters stand between the bars, facing each other. The spotters reach under the low bar with the arm closest to the bar and grasp the performer's wrist with a hand that has been turned so that the palm is facing away from the bars and the thumb is pointing down. The spotters place the other forearm across the gymnast's back as she begins to return to the starting position to help lift her. The hand on the gymnast's wrist is only for kinesthetic awareness of the gymnast's progress. The arm lifting the back should be placed early so that it can assist the gymnast's own momentum rather than lifting after the gymnast has lost momentum.

Common errors:

1. Bending the elbows or knees (symptom: incomplete leg circle ending by hanging by the knee; Figure 8-14).
2. Tucking the head.
3. Failing to shift the weight far forward at the start of the circle.

Connections:

1. Leg circle to a catch on the high bar.
2. Leg circle facing the high bar to a crossed mixed grip on the high bar and a half twist followed by a leg over the low bar. (Figure 8-15).

Figure 8-14
Common Error in Leg Circle

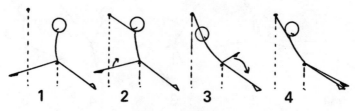

Figure 8-15
Leg Circle 1/2 Turn

Front Hip Circle

(Variations—tuck foward hip circle *without* hands.)

The front hip circle is more difficult to spot than the leg or back hip circles and therefore should be taught after them.

Start: Start in a straight-arm support position, with a good deal of arch and with the hands up and out to the sides (angel or swan balance position).

Procedure: Maintain the arched position while the body begins to rotate in a forward motion around the bar. Just before the body would slip from the bar, forcefully bring the chest to the knees (not knees to the chest, since this counteracts the desired direction of rotation). Bend the knees at the same time. As the chest is being brought to the knees, stretch the arms forward, downward, and then upward to grasp the bar beside the hips in a regular grip. It is very important that the torso and arms are stretched away from the bar for the first third of the rotation of the hip circle. Cues such as "scrape the barrel with the hands," and "stretch" are helpful. As the hands grasp the bar and the chest is close to the thighs and knees, push down on the bar in an effort to arrive at a straight-arm support. At the same time begin to extend the knees and hips into an arched layout position. Finish in a straight-arm support (Figure 8-16).

> *Hint: Encourage your gymnasts to push into an immediate cast from the straight-arm support position. This is helpful in developing a good front hip circle, and it also helps your gymnasts prepare to connect the circle to another movement.*

Spotting: Stand behind the low bar next to the gymnast's left leg. Place your right forearm across her upper calves. You can use your right arm to keep the gymnast from sliding forward off the bar if she begins the tuck too late by spotting the legs and not allowing her legs to move upward. However, once the gymnast has tucked sufficiently to keep the bar at the bend in her hips, release your right arm. Place your left arm under the low bar and then on the gymnast's back. Use your left arm to help provide additional forward rotation to the gymnast as well as to assist her in bringing the chest to the knees for the tuck portion of the circle.

As the gymnast is nearing the completion of the circle, take your now-free right hand and place it across her back to help lift her up toward the bar into the straight-arm support position.

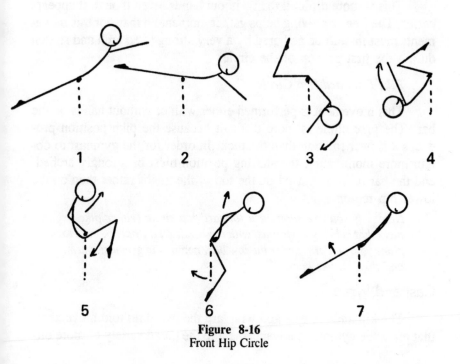

Figure 8-16
Front Hip Circle

Common errors:

1. Failing to bend at the hips soon enough and thus sliding forward off the bar.
2. Failing to wait long enough before bending at the hips and thus losing momentum.
3. Bringing the knees toward the chest rather than the chest toward the knees (symptom: decreased momentum).
4. Not stretching with the arms.
5. Opening into a layout too soon (symptom: feet land on floor and face—or neck or chest, depending on the gymnast's height—moves rapidly and dangerously toward the low bar).

Note: Learning gymnasts often hit the bar with the forearms first and then grasp it with their hands as they finish the movement. The forearms become quite bruised. Taping a small towel or piece of foam rubber around the gymnast's forearm during the learning process can prevent the bruising.

Variations

Tuck Forward Hip Circle with Hands

This is more difficult than without hands, even though it appears easier. The free arm swing helps gather momentum that, for this movement, must instead be gathered by a very strong torso arch and stretch during the first portion of the circle.

Pike Forward Hip Circle

This movement is performed either with or without hands on the bar. The pike circle is more difficult because the pike position produces a slower rotation than the tuck. In order for the gymnast to obtain more momentum, the starting position must be strongly arched, and the bar must be placed on the top of the thighs rather than on the lower hip region.

Note: If you are spotting a forward hip circle (either pike or tuck) that is being performed with the hands on the bar, be sure to place your left arm under the low bar, behind the gymnast's arm, and then on her back.

Cast and Wrap

The kip and the cast and wrap are the two threshold movements that mark the gymnast's advancement to the broad variety of more difficult bar movements. To teach it correctly and completely in a class is often too time consuming.

The initial steps in the progression for the cast and wrap can be taught in a class even though the entire progression is not feasible. So if you decide to expose your class to the fun of the cast and wrap, proceed through Steps 1 and 2 of the progression below. Save the rest of the steps for a club or team.

Step 1—Cast Away (Low Bar)

Start: Straight-arm support; regular grip on the low bar.

Procedure: Pike legs under the low bar as though performing the cast for a back hip circle. Extend the hips and push the body backward and away from the low bar so that a straight line is attained from the hands through the feet at a height about level with the low bar (Figure 8-17, positions 1–4, p. 125).

Spotting: Use four spotters; position two on each side of the gymnast's legs, facing each other. As the gymnast casts back, each spotter catches her by the ribs, hips, or legs, depending on the spotter's location. On the command of the head spotter, the two spotters most distant from the low bar release their hold and set the gymnast's feet on the floor.

Common errors:

1. Arching back and throwing head back. *Correction:* Have gymnast look at a chalk mark on mats about three feet in front of the low bar.
2. Straddling legs (dangerous for last two spotters). *Correction:* Have gymnast hold a rolled-up sock between her ankles during the cast.
3. Having a bend in the elbow or shoulder at the time the spotters catch the gymnast. *Correction:* "Push bar away," "Extend feet toward back wall," "Head level with bar right away."
4. Forgetting to hang onto the bar. Spotters should be prepared for the occasional gymnast who releases the bar.

Step 2—Cast Away (High Bar)

Start: Same as Step 1—straight-arm support, regular grip on the high bar, facing the low bar. Look at the center of the low bar.

Procedure: Same as Step 1.

Note: Emphasize the straight line between hands and feet before the gymnast is caught. If the gymnast is allowed to practice the cast with a bend at the shoulders consistently, she runs a greater risk of her hands slipping off the bar at the bottom of the swing.

Spotting: Same as Step 1.

Note: Because of the gymnast's increased speed (compared to Step 1), the spotters must be prepared to absorb more of her momentum.

Common errors: Same as Step 1, except that the errors are often exaggerated by the longer swing before the gymnast is caught and the gymnast's fear of the added height.

Step 3—Smash and Wrap

The name of this movement sounds gruesome, but students seem to find humor in its descriptiveness.

Start: Face the low bar and jump to a long hang on the high bar with a regular grip.

Procedure: 1. *Adjust the bar.* The spotter should swing the gymnast forward to the low bar. The bar should contact the gymnast in one of two ways: (a) *tummy wrap*—between the navel and the points of the pelvis (anterior superior iliac spines; and (b) *hip wrap*—between the pubic bone and the points of the pelvis. Your taller gymnasts will need to use the tummy wrap if you are using a typical set of stationary bars.

If the bars are contacting too low on the gymnast's body, turn the low bar in, toward the high bar. Conversely, if the contact is too high, turn the bar out, away from the high bar. It may be necessary to lower the low bar one notch if the contact point is still too high after the bar is turned all the way out. Swing and push the gymnast toward the bar to recheck the adjustment. Do not let her try to swing herself into the bar because she will pike before contact and thus inaccurately measure the bar placement. Teach your gymnast how to reset the bars for her next practice session without having to go through the entire measurement process.

2. *The gymnast should follow these instructions:* As your spotter pulls you away from the bar and then pushes your hips into contact with the bar, allow your body to *pike after contact.* When your body is in a *"V" position* (toes pointing to ceiling), *release* the *high bar* and *regrasp the low bar* beside the hips in a regular grip. Finish the rotation around the bar in the same manner as for a regular back hip circle (Figure 8-17, positions 5–9).

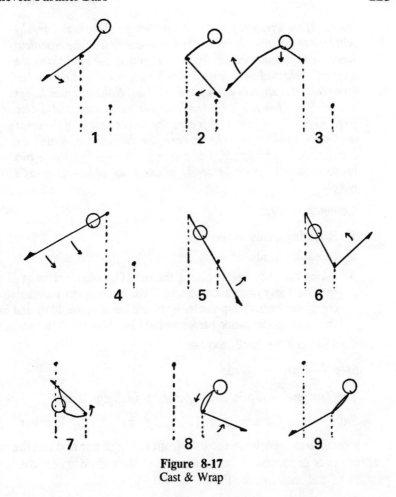

Figure 8-17
Cast & Wrap

Spotting: Use three spotters. Two spotters stand in front of the low bar and spot in the same manner as for a back hip circle. The third spotter stands between the high and low bars and on the left side of the gymnast. The third spotter has the responsibility of pulling the gymnast away from the bar and then pushing her toward the bar by placing her left hand on the front of the gymnast's thighs and her right hand on the gymnast's hips and lower back.

The third spotter should try to hold the gymnast's hips into the bar as long as possible after contact is made. The busy third spotter should try to prevent an early pike (before the bar is contacted) by pushing forward at the gymnast's hips and pulling backward slightly at her thighs. "Belly button to the bar first" is a useful cue.

Note: *If the gymnast pikes early and lets go of the high bar, she will tend to fall directly below the bar—back first. If the miscalculation is sufficiently minor, she will complete the circle with the spotters' help and only complain of hitting her thighs on the bar (symptom of a slightly early hand release). If the gymnast hangs onto the high bar too long, she loses her momentum and is also likely to fall, back first. In this case she will complain, if the error is minor enough to allow her to complete the circle, of hitting the bar very hard with her hips or abdomen. In either case, the two forward spotters must be ready to catch all of the gymnast's weight.*

Common errors:

1. Releasing hands unevenly.
2. Releasing hands too early (before "V" position is attained).
3. Piking the body before hitting the bar. This often occurs at Step 3 because the gymnast doesn't feel she has enough momentum to complete the back hip circle. Reassure her that she does, and have the third spotter work harder to hold her hips into the bar.
4. Releasing the hands too late.

Step 4—Cast and Wrap

The cast and wrap is a combination of Steps 2 and 3.

Start: Straight arm support on high bar, facing low bar.

Procedure: Perform the cast from the high bar and use the momentum thus produced to contact the low bar and complete the wrap portion of the movement (Figure 8-17).

Spotting: Three spotters should be in the same positions as for the smash and wrap (Step 3). The two spotters in front of the low bar will spot the same as for the smash and wrap. The third spotter, instead of swinging the gymnast into the bar from a long hang, will only slow down the gymnast from the cast and then guide her into contact with the low bar. If the cast is very poor, the third spotter may decide to stop the gymnast's forward progress before she hits the low bar in much the same way as the spot for Step 2.

As the gymnast becomes more proficient at the cast and wrap, less interference is needed by the spotters. Remove one of the two forward spotters first, then the spotter behind the low bar, followed finally by the other spotter in front of the low bar.

Common errors:

1. Same as for the Smash and Wrap (Step 3).
2. Being unable to control the momentum during the wrap phase of the movement. *Correction:* Have your gymnast try to "Resist the pike" slightly and "Keep legs from going under the low bar" at the completion of the circle.

Sole Circles and Seat Circles

Sole circles and seat circles are beyond the scope of this book. That is not to say these circles are particularly difficult movements. Rather, they are only difficult to teach to completion in most classes and clubs. As your gymnasts progress to team participation, they should learn these circles.

TRANSITION MOVEMENTS

Transition movements are from one bar to another or from one position to another.

Thigh Roll

The thigh roll is a variation of the thigh roll mount, found on p. 113. The thigh roll, as a transition, is performed from a starting position, with one leg over the low bar and both hands on the high bar (Figure 8-9 [1]).

Stationary Kip

The stationary kip is a variation of the glide kip mount, and is described on p. 116.

Single-Leg Pullover

The single-leg pullover is a variation of the back hip pullover mount, and is described on p. 111.

Double-Leg Stem Rise

The double-leg stem rise—along with the single leg pullover—is an important and basic method of arriving in a straight-arm support on the high bar.

Start: Grasp the high bar in a regular grip facing the low bar, balls of the feet together on the low bar.

Procedure: Tuck knees and hips totally and then begin to move hips forcefully (away from the low bar) by *extending* knees and hips. Pull the hips toward the high bar just as the legs approach complete extension. As the hips approach the high bar, push off of the low bar and swing the legs backward. Finish in a straight-arm support position (Figure 8-18).

Spotting: Two spotters, facing each other, stand between the bars on either side of the gymnast. The spotter on the gymnast's left side places her left hand on the gymnast's left ankle. Her right hand should be placed on the gymnast's hip or lower back. Follow the gymnast as she tucks and as she extends. Push and lift at the hips as she lifts up toward the high bar. The other spotter does the same. The hand on the gymnast's ankle is used to provide the spotter with a kinesthetic warning if the gymnast pushes off with her feet too early. If she does, grasp her around the waist firmly and quickly.

Common errors:

1. Trying to lift the hips up to the high bar before the legs extend. *Correction:* "In, out, and up."
2. Allowing the hips to move upward and over the feet as the body is tucked at the beginning of the movement. *Correction:* "Hips hang low—imagine a cannon ball sitting on your stomach."
3. Taking the feet off the low bar too soon.
4. Leaning backward so that the shoulders never move forward over the high bar.

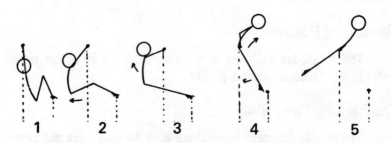

Figure 8-18
Double-Leg Stem Rise

Single-Leg Stem Rise

Start: Start in the same position as for the single-leg pullover, but place the right leg on top of the low bar, with knee straight.

Procedure: Bring the right ankle up to the high bar. Extend the left leg. As the left leg is extending, pull the hips up to the high bar, keeping the right leg close to the bar. The bar should move along the right leg from the ankle to the hip. As the hips approach the high bar, swing the right leg down toward the low bar. As it becomes parallel with the left leg, push off the bar with the left leg and swing both legs, together, backward into a straight-arm support (Figure 8-19).

Spotting: Use one spotter on the left side of the gymnast and spot the same as for a double-leg stem rise.

Common errors:

1. Same as for double-leg stem rise.
2. Allowing the right leg to swing away from the bar rather than proceeding along it as the hips are brought to the bar.

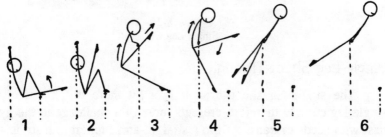

Figure 8-19
Single-Leg Stem Rise

Single-Leg Cut

The leg cut is an easy way for a beginner to change from a straight-arm support to a stride seat, ready to do a leg circle.

Start: Straight-arm support with regular grip.

Procedure: Lift the right leg sideward and upward forcefully and swing it over the low bar. As the straight leg passes over the low bar, remove the right hand momentarily and lean slightly to the left, keeping the left arm straight. As soon as the leg is in front of the bar, regrasp the low bar with the right hand, with elbow straight (Figure 8-20).

Spotting: One spotter is needed. Stand in front of the low bar near the performer's left side. Place your left hand on her upper arm and your right hand on her left wrist (same spotting grip as for the squat vault on beam and horse).

Common errors:

1. Failing to lift right hand until the leg stops, blocked by the hand.
2. Bending the elbows.

Connections:

1. Leg circle.
2. Leg cut dismount.

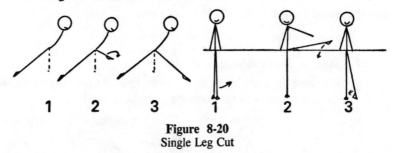

Figure 8-20
Single Leg Cut

Single-Leg Shoot-Through

The single-leg shoot-through is a bit more difficult than the single-leg cut and therefore presents more of a challenge to the gymnast who needs to transfer from a straight-arm support to a stride seat in preparation for a leg circle.

Start: Straight-arm support with regular grip.

Procedure: Cast backward as though you were performing a back hip circle. Just before you reach the height of the cast, quickly tuck leg close to the chest and abduct the scapula while pushing down on the bar. Bring the tucked leg between the hands and over the low bar. As soon as the foot clears the low bar, lift the head and finish in a stride seat, with the weight held off the bar (Figure 8-21).

Spotting: Use two spotters, one in front of the low bar and one behind. The front spotter should spot exactly as though spotting for a single-leg cut. The spotter behind the low bar should stand on the gymnast's left side. Place your left hand on the front of her left thigh and your right hand on the back side of her thigh or calf. As the gymnast's legs move backward during the cast portion of the movement, gently help her to gain height. At the height of the cast, immobilize her left leg until her right foot clears the low bar. Then slowly return her left leg to the bar.

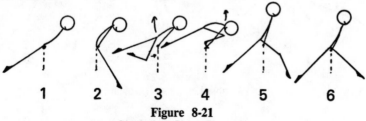

Figure 8-21
Single Leg Shoot-Through

Common errors:

1. Bending the elbows.
2. Waiting until the cast is at its greatest height before beginning to tuck the leg.
3. Looking down at the completion of the movement.
4. Allowing the body weight to rest on the bar as soon as the foot clears the bar.

Connection:

1. Leg circle.
2. Leg cut dismount.

Variation: Double-Leg Shoot-Through

This movement is more advanced than the single-leg shoot-through.

Start: Straight-arm support with regular grip.

Procedure: The procedure is basically the same as for the single leg shoot-through except that both legs tuck rather than just one. A progression you may find helpful is to lower the low bar as low as it will go and then have the gymnast perform a double-leg shoot-through to a standing position in front of the low bar. After this step is mastered, have your gymnast lean back slightly at the completion of passing over the low bar, lift the head, and try to stay on the bar in a straight-legged sitting position (Figure 8-22).

Spotting: Use two spotters, both standing in front of the low bar on either side of the gymnast. Each spotter spots as though she were the front spotter in a single-leg shoot-through.

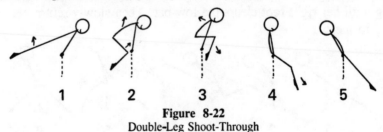

1   2   3   4   5

Figure 8-22
Double-Leg Shoot-Through

DISMOUNTS

Forward Roll over Low Bar

This dismount is an excellent movement for a gymnast to learn the first day she works on the bars. After getting up into a straight-arm support, she can bend over, release her hands, regrasp, and dismount with a forward roll. The gymnast learns that a tight grip is not always needed on the bars, and she also gains familiarity with the bars by being upside down for a moment.

Start: Straight-arm support with a regular grip on the low bar.

Procedure: Pike and momentarily hang on the bar, with the head close to the thighs. Remove hands and regrasp in a reverse grip. Continue the rotation and slide the bar from the hips down to the knees. Step out to the floor (Figure 8-23).

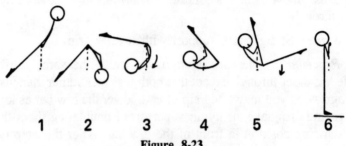

1   2   3   4   5   6

Figure 8-23
Forward Roll Dismount

Spotting: Use one spotter, standing in front of the low bar and to the left side of the performer. After the gymnast is in the pike position, place your right hand on her back and your left hand on her thighs. Assist her rotation and leg control.

Common errors:

1. Allowing the legs to move away from the bar as the body rotates.
2. Incompletely piking.

Variations:

1. Straight-arm support to a swan balance to a pike position for the forward roll without regrasping the bar until the pike is completed.
2. Forward roll over high bar to a long hang with back to low bar. Start with back toward low bar.
3. Same as Variation 2 except once in the long hang perform a half twist to face the low bar by releasing one hand. The body will easily turn away from the released hand.

Skin the Snake

Conceptually the skin the snake is a variation of the forward roll.

Start: Straight-arm support with a regular grip on the high bar, facing the low bar.

Procedure: Pike and grasp the low bar in a reverse grip.

Note: Some beginners feel more confident grasping the low bar with a regular grip and then shifting to a reverse grip afterward.

Bend the elbows and bring the chest down to the low bar while keeping the rest of the body straight. Tuck head under low bar and continue "slithering" down from high to low bars and then finish as though performing a forward roll dismount.

Spotting: Use two spotters. One spotter should stand in front of the gymnast, in front of the low bar. The first spotter cups her hands (palms up) on the performer's shoulders and helps lower her gently to the point where her chest is on the low bar. The spotter then moves to the gymnast's side and spots as though spotting a forward roll dismount. The second spotter should be reasonably tall. The second spotter stands between the bars and underneath the descending gymnast and grasps her hips to help give confidence, slow the descent, and guide the path. The second spotter should move to the gymnast's side as soon as the gymnast's feet pass the high bar.

Common errors:

1. Allowing the back to arch or sag, or piking.
2. Unconsciously trying to catch the high bar with the feet by dorsally flexing the feet as they pass the bar.

Long Hang

This dismount is very easy.

Equipment: Be sure the mats extend at least 8 feet beyond bars.

Start: Long hang from high bar with regular grip and back toward the low bar.

Procedure: Pike, arch, pike. The second pike will produce momentum away from the bars. Release the bar and arch slightly. Then land in a standing position several feet beyond the base of the bar (Figure 8-24).

Spotting: Very little spotting is needed except to provide confidence or assist in and developing amplitude. Spot beyond the high bar, to the side of the gymnast. Place one hand in front of the gymnast's waist and the other on her back.

Connections: Forward roll over high bar to long hang dismount.

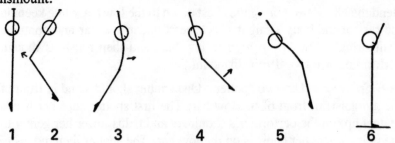

Figure 8-24
Long Hang Dismount

Leg Cut Dismount

This dismount is also called the single-leg flank dismount.

Start: Stride seat on low bar with reverse grisp, facing away from the high bar and with right leg forward. The starting position is identical with that of the leg circle.

Procedure: Lean slightly to the right, placing more of the body weight on the right hand. At the same time lift the left leg sideward and upward over the bar. Join the left and right legs together; turn a quarter turn to the right; and land in a standing position, with the right hand on the low bar and the right side facing the low bar.

Spotting: Use one spotter, who stands in front of the low bar and to the gymnast's right side. The spotter grasps the gymnast's right upper arm with her right hand and the wrist with her left hand.

Common Error: Bending the right arm.

Connection: Leg circle leg cut dismount.

Skin the Cat Dismount

Start: Grasp the high bar with a regular grip, facing the low bar. Put both legs over the low bar, with bent knees together. Hips may be piked (Figure 8-25).

Procedure: Release your grip on the high bar and immediately *regrasp* the *low bar* in a regular grip. Rotate backward using the shoulders as the axis until the feet point toward the mat. Release grip, landing in a standing position.

> *Note: It is often helpful to practice the rotation part a few times before trying the entire movement. In order to practice, stand facing the low bar and about 1 foot away. Grasp the low bar with a regular grip; bend the knees and hips until arms and torso hang directly under the bar. Lift one leg up to the low bar and use the foot to climb through the low bar and the hands. Bring the other leg up to the first. Complete the rotation until the feet rest on the floor.*

Spotting: One spotter is sufficient. Stand between the bars to the left side of the gymnast. As soon as her hands are placed on the low bar, grasp her forearm and wrist.

Variation—Skin the Cat

Start: Sit on the low bar, facing the high bar with a regular grip on the high bar.

Procedure: Slide off the low bar to a momentary long hang position with a slight arch. Immediately pike (prettier) or tuck (easier) both legs up to the high bar. Bring feet through between the high bar and the arms and continue to rotate until the ankles rest on the low bar. Complete the movement with an ankle pivot. To perform the ankle pivot, release the right hand and reach for a spot on the low bar about 6 inches beyond the left ankle. This will result in an automatic turn ending in either a riding seat or a single-leg squat with the left hand on the high bar and the right hand behind the hips on the low bar.

Note: Although this movement involves too much of a slow climbing component to be of any compositional value beyond a beginning routine, it does provide a very useful transition element for beginners.

Spotting: Stand between the bars on the gymnast's left side. Place your right hand on the gymnast's lower back and your left hand on the top of her left thigh. As she slides off the bar, gently push the hips forward and the thigh backward to encourage her to arrive in a long hang position with a small arch. Then shift the left hand to the back of the left thigh and help lift the legs up to the high bar. Once the gymnast's feet pass the high bar, reach for her ankles and insure their gentle landing on the low bar. Then touch (don't just *say*, "Left arm") her left arm and point to a spot 6 inches beyond her right ankle on the low bar and say, "Left hand to low bar."

Note: The body position just before the ankle pivot is awkward, and most gymnasts have difficulty knowing their right from left in an inverted position. Therefore it is necessary to touch the right arm.

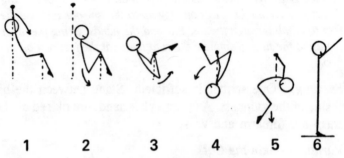

| 1 | 2 | 3 | 4 | 5 | 6 |

Figure 8-25
Skin the Cat Dismount

Underswing Dismount

Start: Straight-arm support with regular grip on the low bar, with back to high bar.

Procedure: Without casting, strongly pike the legs under the bar, and then lean backward. As the torso passes under the low bar with the elbows straight and hips as close to the bar as possible, begin to arch the back to drive feet upward and forward and away from the bars. Release the bar as the body moves away from the bars. Land in a standing position (Figure 8-26).

Spotting: Use three spotters. Two spotters stand in front of the low bar on either side of the gymnast. They spot under the gymnast's thighs and back to help keep her hips close to the bar and to provide some feeling of the flight that the completed movement should have. As the gymnast arches and begins coming down to the floor, shift the hand that had been on her thighs to her abdomen. If she tucks her head or brings her arms down too soon, she will have a lot of forward momentum and the spotter's hand across the abdomen can be used to keep her from falling forward. The third spotter is the "catcher." She should stand 6 feet in front of the low bar and a little to the side of the gymnast's path. If the gymnast has great forward momentum, the third spotter should grasp her around her waist.

Common errors:

1. Failing to arch the back. *Correction:* Put a piece of tape on the under side of the bar and have the gymnast look for it as she passes beneath.
2. Letting the hips drop from the bar. *Correction:* A stronger, more forceful pike is needed.
3. Bringing the hands down or tucking the head upon landing.

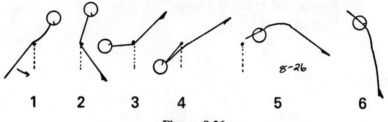

1   2   3   4   5   6

Figure 8-26
Underswing Dismount

A FEW SAMPLE ROUTINES FOR BEGINNERS

Routine 1

1. Straight-arm support on low bar, facing high bar.
2. Single-leg cut.
3. Bring second leg over the bar to join the first.
4. Skin the cat (transition movement, not the dismount.)
5. Stand up on low bar, facing high bar.
6. Forward roll over high bar.
7. Long hang dismount.

Routine 2

1. Thigh roll mount.
2. Optional leg circle facing high bar, leg cut.
3. Skin the cat.
4. Half turn and stem rise or single-leg pullover.
5. Swan.
6. Skin the snake dismount.

Routine 3

1. Back hip pullover mount facing high bar.
2. Back hip circle.
3. Single-leg shoot-through.
4. Leg circle.
5. Swing rear leg over low bar and grasp high bar in regular grip.
6. Single-leg stem rise to straight-arm support on high bar.
7. Forward roll to sitting position on low bar.
8. Skin the cat dismount.

9

Side-horse vaulting

The horse is a very versatile piece of gymnastics equipment. With the pommels in place, the horse functions in men's side-horse pommel work; with the pommels removed the same horse serves men's long horse vaulting and women's side-horse vaulting.

As you prepare the horse for use in women's side-horse vaulting:

1. Remove the pommels.
2. Cover or plug the pommel holes in the top of the body of the horse.

Note: Your gymnasts will be placing their hands correctly on or near these holes and might be severely injured by catching a finger in one of them.

3. Place the horse at least 12 feet away from the wall. As your gymnasts increase the speed of their approaches, the minimum length of your landing area must also be increased. If you have any doubt about the sufficiency of the length of your landing area:

   a. Move the horse farther from the wall, or if this is impossible,
   b. Lean mats against the wall at the end of the landing area and station a spotter near the wall to act as "catcher" to stop the forward progress of any out-of-control landings.

4. Place landing mats (minimum size 6 × 12 feet) in the landing area. Place the leading edge of the mat against the base of the horse Four-inch thick landing mats are best. If a landing mat is unavailable, the best substitute is the use of two 2-inch thick mats stacked on top of each other. Do *not* use 12-inch crash mats for beginners. Their use increases the risk of knee injuries.

5. Place the horse so that its runway is not going to be interrupted by cross traffic.

6. Place the reuther board an appropriate distance in front of the horse. The following should be considered when determining the appropriate distance:

   a. Skill of the gymnast (closer for beginners).

   b. Height of gymnast (closer for shorter gymnasts).

   c. Amount of spring typically obtained by a particular gymnast from the board (closer for gymnasts obtaining less spring).

   d. Type of vault (closer for bent hip, beginning).

Side-horse vaults may be classified into three general groups for conceptual purposes. These groups are:

Bent-hip Vaults

The basic vocabulary of vaults for your gymnasts should come from this category. Bent-hip vaults have little or no preflight, yet they include vaulting mechanics similar to those in the more difficult vaults. Thus they make excellent lead-ups for horizontal layout vaults and inverted vaults.

Horizontal Layout vaults

The position of the body (tuck/squat, pike/stoop, and so on) during these vaults is frequently the same as in the basic group of bent-hip vaults. However, the addition of preflight and after-flight movements increases the challenge of this second group. This group in turn serves as a logical lead-up and prerequisite for gymnasts working on inverted vaults.

Inverted Vaults

A great deal of preflight and after-flight is involved in this group of vaults. Because of this and because of the height and force involved to obtain the inverted position as contact is made with the horse, this group of vaults is seldom part of a beginning or intermediate class in gymnastics and is not included in this book.

DEVELOPING CORRECT TECHNIQUE FOR USE OF THE REUTHER BOARD

The approach is a vital part of all three vaulting groups. A good vault cannot be executed without a good approach and effective use of the reuther board. Therefore, it is a good idea to practice the components of a good approach without having to vault over the horse at the end of the approach. To do this, set up your equipment as shown in Figure 9-1. Remove the horse and push the mat next to the end of the reuther board.

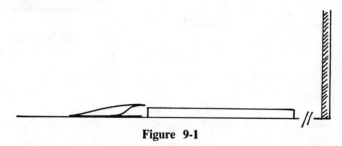

Figure 9-1

Have your gymnasts run repeatedly toward the board, contact the board and land on the mat with two feet. While they are repeating the process over and over, ask them to think about an additional component every few runs.

The components that beginners need to think about are:

1. Land with the toes at least 10 inches behind the end of the board (Figure 9-2).

2. Two-foot take-off from the board.

3. Get on and off the board quickly.

4. Contact the board with the weight being borne through the balls of the feet. (Heels may touch the board but do not bear substantial weight.)

5. Contact the board with *almost* straight knees.

6. Take a long, low hurdle. (The last step before contacting the board should be several feet from the end of the board.)

7. As the gymnast leaves the board, her arms should go up.

8. Hit the board with force.

9. The body should be in line and leaning a bit back as the board is contacted.

10. Stretch in the air following contact with the board and land with balance.

After the components of a good approach and contact with the board have been mastered, replace the horse between the board and mat. Have your gymnast proceed through the following skills.

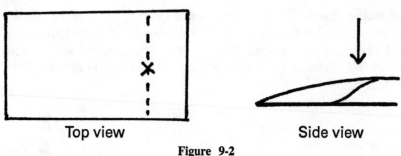

Top view	Side view

Figure 9-2

Shin Mount

Note that *mount* means that the body stops on the horse.

Board: 1 to 1 ½ feet away from the horse.

Approach: A short approach of 2–4 steps is all that is needed for this mount.

Contact:

1. Place hands shoulder-width apart on top of the horse with fingers pointing toward the landing area. Extend elbows (Figure 9-3).
2. Lift the hips.
3. Tuck legs and land gently with the shins on the saddle (middle) of the horse while the hands remain in contact with the horse.

Landing: Climb off the horse onto the landing mat. The shin mount is sometimes taught with a jumping dismount using arm swing to gain height. The jumping dismount has substantial risk and has very little redeeming value and so should be avoided or postponed until the gymnast has more confidence and more skill.

Spotting: The Standard Spot

Stand behind and a bit to the neck or croup ends of the horse as shown in Figure 9-4. Face the gymnast and reach for the gymnast's arm as soon as possible. Use the hand closest to the middle of the horse to grasp the upper arm of the gymnast. The other hand grasps the wrist (Figure 9-5).

Your job as spotter is to give the gymnast confidence and to prevent the shoulders or head from hitting the mat if the gymnast trips, leans forward, or bends her elbows. You should also be able to help the gymnast land in a standing position. Do not release the gymnast until she has successfully climbed off the horse and is on the landing mat. Remember, beginners are likely to do the unexpected simply because they are inexperienced.

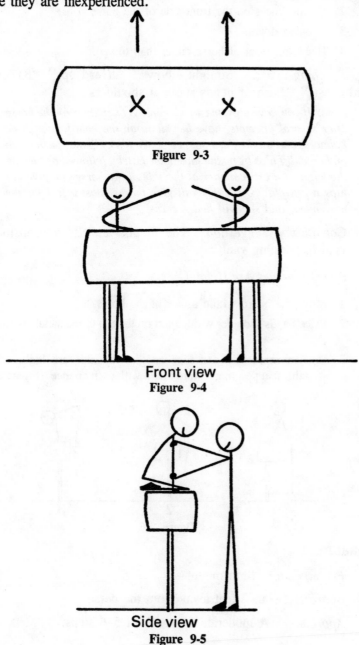

Figure 9-3

Front view
Figure 9-4

Side view
Figure 9-5

Common errors:

1. Bending elbows.
2. Hitting knees on the front side of the horse.
3. Looking down.
4. Hands on front of horse rather than top.

Teaching cues: "Straight elbows," "Head up," "Knees toward chest," "Push of hands starts at shoulders"

Note: If you have a gymnast who can't get her shins on the horse after several attempts, have her stand on the board, take three bounces, and on the third bounce, extend her elbows, push down on horse, lift hips by piking hips immediately, followed by tucking the knees. An extra spotter at the side of the horse can give her hips a little lift. Often this will give the gymnast a feel for the movement, and she will find success.

Conditioning suggestion: The hip pike and elbow extension are both vital to learning vaulting.

Board Bounces Are Helpful

1. Move the board within a foot of the horse.
2. Place hands shoulder width apart on the top of the saddle portion of the horse.
3. Bounce repeatedly and pike so that the hips are high, elbows straight, feet pointing toward board with each bounce. (Figure 9-6.)

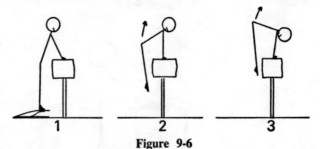

Figure 9-6

Squat Mount

Prerequisite: Shin mount.

Board: 1½ to 2 feet away from the horse.

Approach: A moderate approach of 5–6 steps.

Contact: The contact is the same as for the shin mount except the balls of the feet will contact the saddle of the horse rather than the shins.

Landing: Climb off the horse (Figure 9-7).

Common errors: Same as shin mount.

Teaching cues: "Push," "Elbows straight," "Push from shoulders," "Hips up," "Look up!"

Figure 9-7
Squat Mount

Squat Vault

Vault means that only the hands contact the horse. This is the first true vault (no stop) in the progression. It serves as the mechanical basis for all other vaults, so it must be carefully and correctly learned.

The shin mount, squat mount, and squat vault all involve similar contact and spotting techniques. In classes vaulters practicing any of the three movements can be easily intermixed.

Prerequisites: Shin mount, squat mount.

Board: Two feet away from horse, minimum. As the gymnast becomes more comfortable with the vault and as the preflight increases, the board should be pushed farther and farther away from the horse a few inches at a time.

Contact: Same as Squat Mount, except the feet do not touch the horse.

Repulsion: Before the knees pass in front of a line between the elbows, the hands (with elbows straight) push away from the horse, forcing the shoulders and upper torso upward. The arms continue upward as the body extends vertically in after-flight (Figure 9-8).

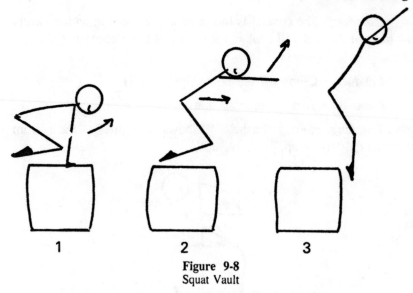

Figure 9-8
Squat Vault

Landing: Land on two feet with knees slightly bent to absorb the momentum. As soon as the momentum is absorbed, extend the knees and demonstrate a balanced position.

Note: Gymnastics jargon for landing with balance is to "stick the land." The squat vault is a good place to start learning to stick every landing.

Common errors:

1. Leaving the hands in contact with the horse too long often results in landing with an arched back—injuries might occur.
2. Failing to drive the shoulders upward during the repulsion phase.
3. Incomplete body extension prior to landing.

Teaching cues: "Look up," "Shoulder up," "Lift chest," "Hands off fast."

Spotting: Standard spot.

Preflight Development

As your gymnast becomes skilled in the bent-hip squat vault, she should practice some or all of the following to develop preflight.

1. Increase distance of board from horse. This starts to develop a stretched body position prior to contacting the horse. As the board is moved back, the starting place for the approach also needs to be moved back. It may be helpful to have each gymnast place a piece of tape on the floor at her starting spot. She can then move the exact starting spot backward as needed. This is also a good time to count the steps of your gymnast's approach and remind her to keep the number consistent. Most *full* approaches involve 11 to 13 steps. Also watch for board contacts that are too close to the end of the board.

2. *Buck-ups*. A buck-up does not involve a mount or vault. A buck-up practices only the approach, preflight, and contact.

Board: 3 to 5 feet from horse.

Approach: Moderate. Contact the board, leaning slightly back. This will produce the desired lift-off from the board (up and slightly forward; Figure 9-9).

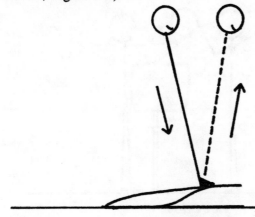

Figure 9-9

Contact: Reach up and over an imaginary horizontal line about 5 feet above the floor between the board and horse. The body should be stretched. Contact the horse with straight elbows, torso, and legs. The feet should be higher than the head. This is where the buck-up ends. The momentum is absorbed by the spotters. Pike to return to a standing position on the floor.

Spotting: Three spotters are needed.

Spotter 1. Stand behind the horse on the landing mat. Your job is to stop the gymnast's forward momentum by placing your hands on her shoulders (Figure 9-10).

Spotters 2 and 3. Stand between the board and the horse, one on either side of the saddle. (Leave room for the gymnast in between.) Face each other. As the gymnast leaves the board on her way to the horse, place one arm under her rib cage and the other on her thighs, and lift. Then gently lower the gymnast to the floor by releasing her thighs while continuing to give her rib cage some support.

Common errors:

1. Aiming directly at the horse rather then going up and over the imaginary line.
2. Bending elbows.
3. Tucking the head.

Teaching cues: "Up and over," "Lean back on the board," "Elbows straight," "Stretch," "Head up."

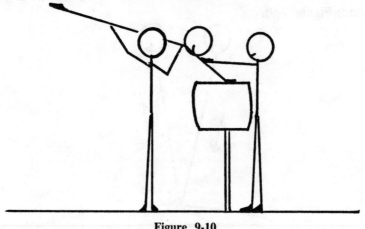

Figure 9-10
Buck-Ups

Stoop Mount

Besides being a good lead-up for the stoop vault, the stoop mount helps your gymnasts learn to lift their hips and thus aids in the perfection of the squat vault.

Prerequisites: Squat mount; hamstring flexibility.

Board: 2½ to 3 ½ feet away from the horse.

Approach: Moderate.

Contact: Same as for squat mount, except the knees are extended rather than in a tuck position (Figure 9-11).

Landing: Jump forward off the horse and lift chest to land on the mat with two feet.

Spotting: Standard spot.

Common errors:

1. Bending knees
2. Tucking head, which produces a feeling of falling forward.

Teaching cues: "Look Up," "Knees straight from board," "Pike," "Hips up."

Conditioning suggestion: A good deal of hamstring flexibility is needed for this movement.

Figure 9-11
Stoop Mount

Stoop Vault

Prerequisites: Squat vault, stoop mount, hamstring flexibility.

Board: 3 to 5 feet away from the horse.

Approach: Full.

Contact: Same as for squat vault, except body is in a pike rather than tuck position.

Repulsion: Before the feet pass in front of the hands, the hands push away from the horse, forcing the shoulders and upper torso upward. The arms continue upward as the body extends vertically in after-flight.

Common errors: Late repulsion with the hands; failing to drive shoulders upward during the repulsion phase; incomplete body extension during after-flight.

Teaching cues: "Push-off early," Extend during after-flight," "Knees straight."

Spotting: Standard spot.

The following four movements: flank vault, front vault, straddle mount and straddle vault, provide additional bent-hip vaults for your gymnasts to work on while perfecting the basic skills of vaulting. However, they are not as effective as lead-ups for the development of preflight techniques as are the squat and stoop vaults. Their benefits come from the broadening of the vocabulary of vaults on a beginning level. In most classes, the advancement to preflight (horizontal and layout) vaults is a slow one. A variety of movements keeps up the interest while allowing the class to progress at an appropriate speed.

Flank Vault (Side Vault)

Prerequisites: Shin mount, courage mount.

Board: 2 to 3 feet away from the horse.

Approach: Moderate.

Contact: Same as all previous mounts and vaults. As soon as the feet leave the board, both legs and hips are lifted to one side so that the body is in the position illustrated in Figure 9-12 as it passes over the horse.

Repulsion: Before the hips pass over the horse, the hand on the side of the elevated legs lifts upward, with the elbow straight (Figure 9-12).

Landing: As soon as the hips pass the horse, the body pivots at the shoulder (on the side where the hand is contacting the horse), downward into a vertical position. Land on two feet, back facing the horse.

Common errors:

1. Leaving both hands on the horse too long.
2. Landing with the side toward the horse instead of the back.
3. Knees bent during preflight.
4. Lifting hips very high over the horse while failing to lift the feet (characterized by a pike position while over the horse).
5. Landing on the side of the reuther board in preparation for lifting legs to the same side.

Teaching cues: "Knees straight off the board," "Lift one arm," "Land with the back to the horse," "Legs horizontal."

Spotting: Standard spot. Only one spotter can be used, and she must spot on the side away from the gymnast's legs.

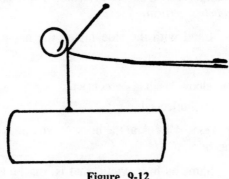

Figure 9-12
Flank Vault

Front Vault

Prerequisite: Squat mount.

Board: 2 to 3 feet away from the horse.

Approach: Moderate.

Contact: Both legs will pass over the same side of the horse during the front vault. If the legs are going over the croup (right side of horse), the gymnast's hands should be placed:

1. Left—same as for squat vault.
2. Right—turned to point toward the left hand (Figure 9-13).

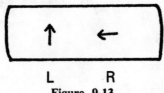

L   R
Figure 9-13
Hand Placement for Front Vault

Repulsion: The body will pass over the horse with the face and front of body toward the top of the horse (unlike the flank vault, where the side passes over the horse). Both legs will be extended horizontally in the same direction to the side of the horse. As soon as the body passes over the horse, pike, bringing the feet down for the landing while at the same time lifting the chest and pushing down and away with the turned hand.

Note: As skill increases, the body can move above horizontal until it approaches vertical.

Landing: Land with the side facing the horse.

Common errors:

1. Extreme elbow bending on contact.
2. Legs below horizontal.

Teaching cues: "Look at the horse as you pass over it," "Land with side to the horse."

Spotting: Same as flank vault; that is, on the arm opposite the lifted legs.

Straddle Mount

Prerequisites: Shin mount, squat mount, squat vault, adductor and hamstring flexibility.

Board: 2 to 3 feet away from the horse.

Approach: Moderate.

Contact: The hand position is the same as for the squat vault (Figure 9-14). As soon as the feet leave the board, pike and straddle the legs while, with straight elbows, pushing down on the horse and lifting the hips. Place the feet with knees straight on either end of the horse. Then climb off.

Common errors:

1. Bending knees.
2. Failing to look up.

Teaching cues: "Knees straight from board," "Look up."

Spotting: Standard spot.

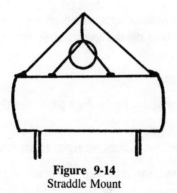

Figure 9-14
Straddle Mount

Straddle Vault

Although the straddle vault is frequently used in beginning gymnastics, it produces a substantial number of knee injuries. These injuries occur because the gymnast lightly catches one foot or toe on the horse as she goes over. This causes her to land off balance with all the weight on one leg. Thus the straddle vault needs exceptional spotting to be safely employed in a beginning program. Unfortunately, it is almost impossible to provide such spotting. Therefore it is recommended that the straddle vault be included in your beginning gymnastics program only if you use a vaulting buck. A buck is a horse with only the saddle portion. Since it is narrow (no croup and no neck), there is nothing for the gymnast to trip on.

Prerequisites: Squat vault, straddle mount, hamstring and adductor flexibility.

Board: 2 to 3 feet away from the horse.

Approach: Moderate.

Contact: Same as squat vault. As soon as feet leave the board, begin to straddle the legs.

Repulsion: Push the buck away with the hands with straight elbows before the legs pass in front of the hands. At the same time, lift the chest, extend the body vertically, and adduct the legs.

Landing: Two feet, back to back.

Spotting: Standard spot. Immediately step backward while maintaining your grasp on the gymnast so that the gymnast's legs do not hit you.

Common errors:

1. Bending the knees as the legs pass over the buck.
2. Failing to lift the head.

Teaching cues: "Knees straight from board," "Look up."

All of the above mounts and vaults are members of the bent-hip group. Most of them can also be performed as members of the horizontal and layout group. (The squat vault and stoop vault are particularly effective members of both groups.)

Although inverted vaults might seem challenging to your gymnasts, remember that inverted vaults increase the possibility of injury. Thus it is vital to master the bent-hip and horizontal and layout groups first.

10

Balance beam

The ultimate goal of a balance beam performer is to produce the same freedom of movement found in floor exercise routines. The 4-inch width and nearly 4–foot height of the beam make the achievement of this goal inherently difficult.

A basic principle for effective and safe development of balance beam movements is:

Try it first on the floor, then the low beam, the medium beam, and finally the high beam.

THE EQUIPMENT

Beams

Wooden beams develop gouges and splinters easily if not cared for. The newer, covered beams can be cut and ripped. So prevent other gymnastics equipment (including other beams) from bumping into your beams.

Mats

Adequate, nonoverlapping mats are needed. The higher the beam, the wider the matted area should be.

Location

Beams require a lot of room, particularly on the sides. As the beam's height is increased, the falling gymnast could more easily run into nearby equipment. When the beam is at competition height, there should be at least 10 feet between beams.

Even though beams may be placed quite close (end-to-end) during the first few days of beginning beam work, it is very important to provide extensive end room (a minimum of 12 feet) whenever gymnasts are working on end dismounts.

Beam Accessories

Commercially produced pads that cover about 3 feet of beam and attach under it with Velcro strips, are available and quite useful (for example, for forward rolls). If you have a tight budget you might want to make your own vertebrae pad. To do this, take a snugly fitting (on you, not the beam) hooded sweatshirt and sew a 4–5-inch-wide fabric pocket from midback up to the head. Insert a piece of foam rubber into the pocket.

BEAM ACTIVITIES

Beam movements may be categorized into the following eight categories:

1. Mounts.
2. Locomotor skills.
3. Turns.
4. Poses.
5. Jumps.
6. Leaps.
7. Tumbling and acrobatics.
8. Dismounts.

Mounts

Straight-Arm Support Mount

This mount is also called a crotch seat mount.

Equipment: Beam should be at least waist high.

Start: From the side of the beam, place hands on top of the beam, 6 inches to 1 foot apart. Fingers should point toward the far side of the beam, and elbows should be straight. Hips will be in contact with the side of the beam (Figure 10-1).

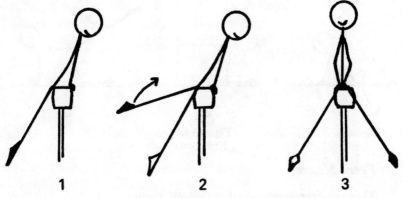

Figure 10-1
Straight Arm Support Mount

Procedure: Push down on the beam; lift one leg sideward up and over the beam, while turning the torso in the direction of the stationary leg. End in a sitting position, with one leg on each side of the beam.

Common error: Bending elbows.

Connections:

1. V-sit (Figure 10-2).
2. Step up (Figure 10-3).
3. Knee scale (Figure 10-4).

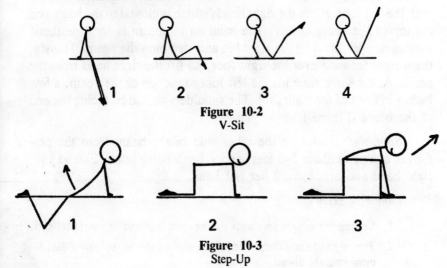

Figure 10-2
V-Sit

Figure 10-3
Step-Up

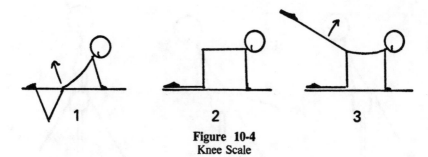

Figure 10-4
Knee Scale

Fence Mount

This is sometimes called a step-on mount.

Equipment: Arrange the board and beam as shown in Figure 10-5.

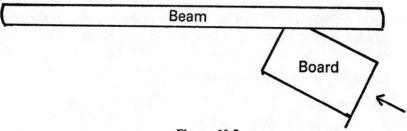

Figure 10-5
(Top View) Board Placement for Fence Mount

Procedure: Take a step or two before stepping on the board with the left foot. Place the right hand (which is closest to the beam) on the top of the beam lightly. The hand on the beam is for kinesthetic awareness, not lift. Lift the right leg and step onto the beam. Transfer the weight forward over the right foot and lift the right hand from the beam. At the same time lift the left foot to the top of the beam, a few inches in front of the right foot. The shoulders should be facing the end of the beam (Figure 10-6).

Spotting: Stand on the other side of the beam from the performer at a point about 2–3 feet beyond her landing point. Extend your right hand and arm toward her left hand.

Common errors:

1. Letting the weight stay back on the right foot and/or the right hand.
2. Turning the shoulders to the right side of the beam rather than facing straight ahead.

Connections:

1. Perform an immediate squat pivot turn to the right.
2. Carry the momentum to an immediate stand (with or without body wave).

Variations:

1. Without hand contact.
2. On the end of the beam.

Figure 10-6
Fence Mount

Squat mount

Equipment: Arrange the board and beam as shown in Figure 10-7.

Procedure and spotting: Same as squat vault.

Helpful hint: The gymnast's shins are easily bruised while learning the squat mount. Hockey shin guards or a towel wrapped around each shin help.

Connection: From the squat position, lift the hands from the beam and twist as in a squat pivot turn to face the end of the beam. The turn can end in either a squat or a stand with or without a body wave.

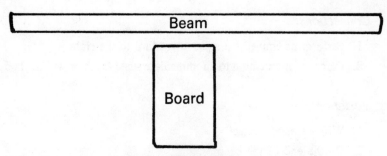

Figure 10-7
(Top View) Board Placement for Squat Mount

Straddle Mount

This mount on the beam is the same as the straddle mount on the horse. The straddle mount is a bit more difficult to balance than the squat mount.

Connection:

Twist the torso to a lunge or a split.

Wolf Mount

Perform the wolf mount in the same way as the straddle or squat mounts, except that one leg is in a squat position between the hands and the other leg is in a straddle position outside the hands (Figure 10-8).

Figure 10-8
Wolf Mount

Riding Seat Mount

Equipment: Same as the fence mount.

Procedure: Begin as though performing the fence mount. After the right hand is placed on the beam, the right leg is lifted up and over the beam, followed by the left leg. The hips are lifted only to the level of the beam. Land sitting on the beam, with both legs on the opposite side from the reuther board (Figure 10-9).

Spotting: Stand on the opposite side of the beam from the reuther board. Grasp the performer's right upper arm as she places her hand on the beam.

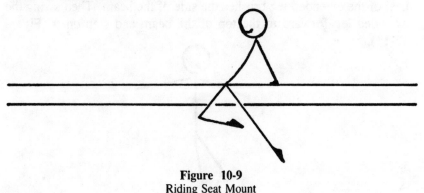

Figure 10-9
Riding Seat Mount

Locomotor Skills

Walk

Walk forward and backward. Practice walking on the beam to become comfortable with the narrowness and height. Practice various arm movements, body alignments, and head positions. Among the points to emphasize are:

1. Keep forward foot and leg extended until the toe touches the beam.
2. Focus the eyes on the end of the beam rather than on the feet.
3. Turn out (laterally rotate) the legs from the hips. This will result in a better looking line of the leg and a foot contact that is on the diagonal (Figure 10-10). A diagonal foot contact provides better balance.
4. Toe touches first.
5. Use arms for balance but don't carry them horizonatally out to the side.
6. When walking backward, make sure the foot is on the beam before puting weight on it.

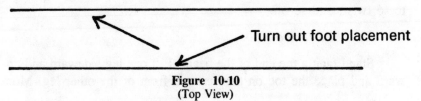

Turn out foot placement

Figure 10-10
(Top View)

Dip Walk

This is also called a plié walk. Bend the supporting leg while the heel of the extended leg brushes the side of the beam. Then swing the extended leg forward to the top of the beam and step on it (Figure 10-11).

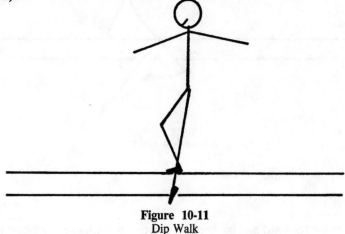

Figure 10-11
Dip Walk

Chassé

Step, close, step.

Waltz

Down up, up.

Step-Hop

Experiment with various leg lifts, such as forward and bent with knee turned out, leg straight, leg straight and extended backwards.

Slide Walk

Stand facing the side of the beam, slide left foot to the left; bring the right foot next to the left. Add interest with bent knees, body wave, torso twist, and so on.

Ronde de Jambe Walk

Stand facing the end of the beam. Lift one leg sideward and upward and place the toe on the beam in front of the other leg. More interest can be added by bending both knees just as the elevated leg begins to descend to the beam, followed by an immediate straightening of the legs. Both legs need to be turned out (laterally rotated), especially during the momentary bent-leg pose.

Running Steps

Take running steps forward on the beam.

Note: Locomotor skills, once learned, should be mixed and varied within a routine. An entire beam length of step-hops or waltz steps should definitely be avoided.

Turns

As soon as your gymnasts have mastered at least one mount and a few locomotor skills, teach them a few turns so that they can put together a combination of movements that involves more than one length of the beam.

Standing Pivot Turn

Stand with one foot in front of the other, close together. Rise up on toes and face the opposite direction by turning toward the back foot. As you go up on your toes at the beginning of the turn, raise both arms over your head. At the completion of the turn, drop arms and drop onto heels.

Squat Pivot Turn

Perform the standing pivot turn except start, turn, and end in a squat position. The *thighs should touch* all the time during the turn.

Variation: Start in a squat and move to a standing position as the turn is made, or vice versa.

Battement Tourney

This is also called a forward kick turn.

Kick the right leg forward as you pivot to your left on the left leg. Complete the turn, facing the opposite end of the beam, with the weight still on the left foot, the right extended backward (Figure 10-12).

Note: This turn is completed with the right backward leg elevated from the beam. This makes balancing a bit tricky.

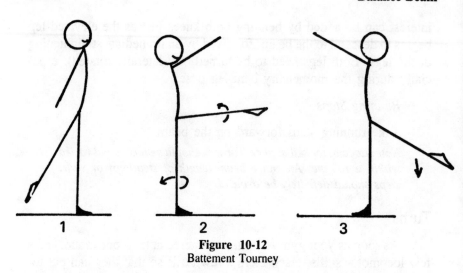

Figure 10-12
Battement Tourney

Back Kick Turn

Stand on the beam with the left leg in front of the right. Kick the right leg forward and then backward. As the right leg moves backward, turn to your right by pivoting on the left foot. Complete the turn by placing the now-forward leg on beam (Figure 10-13).

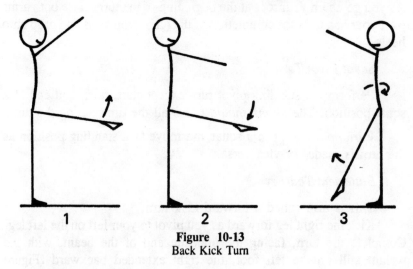

Figure 10-13
Back Kick Turn

Arabesque Turn

Step forward onto right foot and turn torso so that right shoulder is also forward. Swing shoulder to the right and pivot on the right foot to the right while leaving the left leg to trail behind. Complete the turn, facing the other end of the beam, with left foot still behind (Figure 10-14).

Variations: Half-and-half turn. Immediately at the completion of the arabesque, turn, bring the left foot in front of the right (close to the left), and perform a standing pivot turn to the right. This turn appears to be a full turn even though it is much easier.

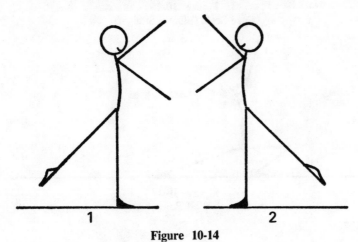

Figure 10-14

Poses

Poses are positions that are held momentarily on the beam. There are no set rules requiring only particular poses, so those your students create are often the best ones (Figures 10-15 through 10-23).

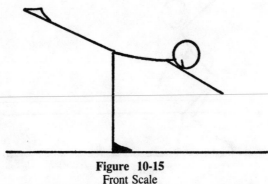

Figure 10-15
Front Scale

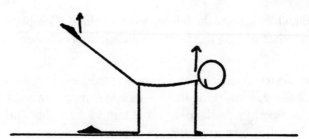

Figure 10-16
Knee Scale (Elbows Straight)

Figure 10-17
Wolf Pose

Figure 10-18
V-Sit

Figure 10-19
Abstract Pose

Figure 10-20
Swan Balance

Figure 10-21
Single-Leg Squat

Figure 10-22
Riding Seat

Figure 10-23
Croisé

Jumps

Beginners should glance at their feet during jumps and leaps to make sure that at least one foot comes in contact with the beam. For other categories of movements, however, the eyes generally should be focused on the end of the beam.

Standing Jump

Start: Same as for a standing pivot turn.

Procedure: Jump and bring legs as close together as possible while in the air. Land in starting position. Remember to absorb the downward force of the landing by slightly bending the knees (Figure 10-24).

Variations of Standing Jump

Squat-to-Squat Jump

Start: Squat with one foot slightly in front of other (Figure 10-25).

Stand, Squat-to-Squat Jump

Start: Stand with one foot slightly in front of other (Figure 10-26).

Figure 10-24
Standing Jump

Figure 10-25
Squat-to-Squat Jump

Figure 10-26
Squat-to-Stand Jump

Squat to a Stand

Start in a squat, jump, and end in a standing position.

Tuck Jump

At the height of any of the previous jumps, tuck the knees and bring the heels in to a momentary contact with the hips. Land in either a stand or a squat position. This is another jump that looks harder than it is (Figure 10-27).

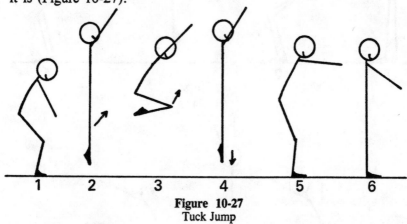

Figure 10-27
Tuck Jump

Two-to-One Jump

Start as in a standing pivot turn. Jump up and forward with the legs straight but, unlike the standing jump, separate the legs forward and backward. Land on the forward leg in a momentary, low arabesque or immediately bring the rear leg forward and take a step (Figure 10-28).

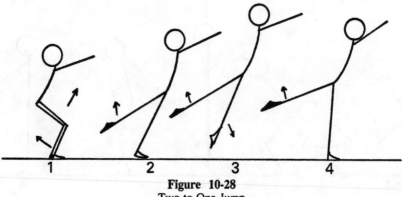

Figure 10-28
Two-to-One Jump

Two-to-Two Jump

Perform in the same manner as the two-to-one jump, but keep the legs together and land with both feet. This can also be done in a squat position.

Leaps

See Chapter 7 for additional information on leaps.

Stride Leap

This is sometimes called a split leap when performed with good amplitude.

Hitch Kick

This leap is sometime called a scissor kick.

Cat Leap

The cat leap is sometimes categorized as a variation of the hitch kick. The mechanics of the cat leap are quite similar to the hitch kick, except that both knees are bent in the air and turned out. To add interest to the cat leap, a slight rounding of the back and contraction of the torso are frequently employed (Figure 10-29).

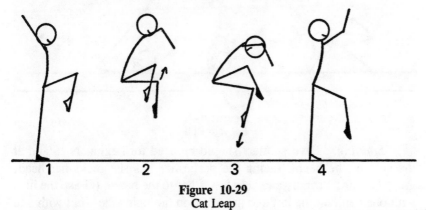

Figure 10-29
Cat Leap

Stag Leap

A stag leap is shown in Figure 7-26.

Cabriole

The cabriole is shown in Figure 7-28.

Tumbling and Acrobatics

Theoretically any tumbling or acrobatic movement that can be performed on the floor can be done on the beam. Those appropriate for beginners to intermediates are discussed below.

Forward Roll

Start: After trying the forward roll on the floor, stand on the beam in a squat position, with feet together. Place hands on top of beam, fingers down the sides, knees inside elbows.

Procedure: Shift the weight to the hands while lifting the hips above the head. Bend the elbows, tuck the head, and place the back of the head or neck (depending on neck flexibility) on the beam. Head may touch in front of or behind the hands. As soon as the head and neck touch the beam, immediately shift the hands to the bottom of the beam and squeeze the elbows together, pulling with the hands to keep the body on the beam.

Note: Once the roll is mastered, the shifting of the hands may be omitted.

As the roll proceeds, keep your feet on the beam as long as possible, thus yielding a straight-legged, piked position for a momentary portion of the roll (Figure 10-30).

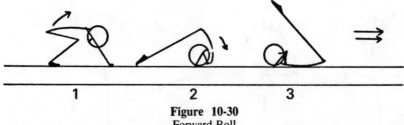

1	2	3

Figure 10-30
Forward Roll

Spotting: Two spotters should be used for beginners. Stand at the side of the beam, facing the performer. As she tucks her head, grasp her hips strongly and help lower her to the beam. (Grasp the hips with one hand on the left and the other on the right side—not with one hand on the lower back and the other on the thighs).

As she continues to roll, direct her hips until her hips contact the beam. Then use your body to keep her from rolling off the beam sideward and place the hand that is closest to the beam over her and grasp the opposite hip to keep her from rolling off the beam on the far side.

The portion of the roll where the gymnast is on her back on the beam is not a stable point. She needs spotting throughout the roll, not just the initial stages.

Common errors:

1. Failure to keep elbows close together and pull on the bottom of the beam after the head and neck touch the beam.
2. When the forward roll is performed for competition, the gymnast should not stop until she arrives at squat.
3. Letting feet leave the beam too early. (The feet should stay on beam until back of head is on the beam. Extend legs to accomplish this.)

Connections:

1. Straddle the beam and swing legs down and backward and then upward to a squat position or knee scale.
2. V-sit.
3. Single-legged squat.
4. Squat position, then to a stand.

Back Shoulder Roll

Start: Start in a supine position on the beam. Place the head to one side of the beam and look down the length of the beam. Hands are placed beyond the head in one of three grips:

1. Both hands grasping the bottom of the beam.
2. One hand grasping the bottom of the beam and the other on top of the beam, with fingers down the side of the beam.
3. Both hands on top of the beam, with fingers down the side of the beam.

Procedure: Lift legs to chest in a tuck or pike position (tuck is easier, pike prettier) and continue rolling over the shoulder until head and torso can be lifted upward. Place one knee on the beam close to the hands and shift hands to the top of the beam to help push the torso upward. Eyes spot the end of the beam during the roll and shift to the other end as the roll is completed (Figure 10-31).

Spotting: Use two spotters at first, one on each side of the beam at the hip of the performer, facing her head. Help balance the performer as she positions her head. Then as she starts to roll, grasp her hips and help her roll by lifting and balancing. Help the performer "find" the beam with her knee.

Common errors:

1. Failure to stay in either a tight tuck or a sharp pike while rolling backward.
2. Forgetting to use hands to push and pull in order to maintain balance.
3. Not spotting the end of the beam.
4. Allowing the elbows to wander out of line.
5. Letting the legs move away from their correct position directly over the beam.

Connections:

1. Knee scale.
2. Squat, squat turn, and stand.
3. Single-leg squat.

Note: The back shoulder roll is not a quick movement and is thus not a good component for more than a beginning routine. But it is easier for most gymnasts to perform than an over-the-head back roll and does provide a good lead-up for learning other types of back rolls.

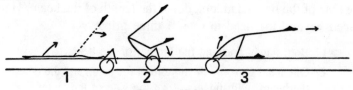

Figure 10-31
Back Shoulder Roll

Back Roll (Over-the-Head)

Start: Assume a supine position, with the hands on the beam beyond the head. The thumbs should be pointing toward the head. A more advanced starting position that should be practiced after the roll itself is mastered is to begin in a squat position and roll directly back into the roll itself.

Procedure: Tuck the legs and perform a back tuck roll in the same manner as you would perform one on the floor.

Spotting: Same as back shoulder roll.

Common errors: Same as back shoulder roll.

Connections: Same as back shoulder roll. The back roll is harder to perform than the back shoulder roll because it is difficult to get over the head with the small amount of momentum generated on the beam. The lower the gymnast can get her hips at the completion of the roll, the easier it is to get over the head.

English Handstand

This movement is also called a three-quarter handstand.

Prerequisite: Handstand on the floor.

Start: Stand on the beam, facing one end, left foot slightly in front of the right.

Procedure: Bend at the waist, placing hands on the top of the beam, with the thumbs and heels of the hands together and fingers grasping the sides. At the same time kick up the right leg, followed quickly by the left, and arrive in a momentary three-quarter handstand position. Bring the right leg (for a switch handstand) or the left leg (for a regular handstand) down to the beam, followed by the other leg. Watch the beam during the contact of the first foot.

Spotting: When this movement is being practiced on the floor or low beam, spot in the same manner as a regular handstand on the floor. When the performer is on the high beam, face the gymnast as you place one hip against the beam. Pile up mats if needed. As she kicks up into the handstand, reach for her hips, shoulders, or upper back to help balance and prevent the unlikely event of the gymnast overbalancing due to kicking up too hard.

Common errors:

1. Not kicking up into a straight body position from shoulders to feet.
2. Allowing the shoulders to travel forward instead of remaining directly over the hands.
3. Arching the back to absorb the kicking motion instead of allowing the body to approach the vertical.

Dismounts

Pirouette Dismounts

These dismounts are very easy.

Start: Stand on the beam with feet close together.

Procedure: Jump with extended legs held close together. Execute a half turn in the air and land next to the beam with your hand on top of the beam for balance.

Fence Dismount

This dismount is also called a push-up dismount.

Start: Get into a push-up position on the beam. A knee scale is a good preceding movement.

Procedure: Keep elbows and body straight as you drop the right leg below the level of the beam. Then bring the right leg up again, providing a bit of upward momentum as it meets and rises with the left leg. Pike at the hips as both legs begin to descend to the floor. Land with feet together and left hand on beam. Landing will be on the right side of the beam (Figure 10-32).

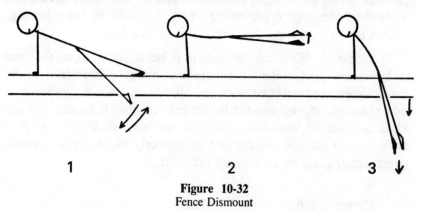

Figure 10-32
Fence Dismount

Spotting: Stand adjacent to the gymnast's waist on the side of the beam opposite to where the gymnast will land (also opposite to the side of the swinging leg). Place your left hand under the gymnast's rib cage and your right hand under the gymnast's left thigh.

Common errors:

1. Arching the back and absorbing all the lift rather than having the legs and hips lift.
2. Twisting and landing facing the beam (The gymnast should land with her side to the beam.)

English Handstand Dismount

Start: Same as english handstand as a tumbling movement (discussed earlier in this chapter).

Procedure: Same as english handstand, except at the height of the leg swing, keep both legs together as you descend and twist slightly so that the landing position is with the side to the beam and about a foot away from the beam.

Round-off Dismount

This dismount can be performed in the middle of the beam (sometimes called a Wendy dismount), but it is easier to spot and perform from the end of the beam. The description below is for an end dismount.

Start: Stand facing the end of the beam, with the right foot forward, about 3–4 feet away from the end of the beam.

Procedure: Perform a standing round-off with hands together, close to end of beam. Land facing beam. Hands will leave the beam a moment before you land.

Spotting: Stand on the side of the beam to the standing gymnast's right but about 2 feet beyond the end of beam. As she places her hands on the beam, grasp her upper left arm (second hand down) with your inverted left hand. As her torso begins to descend, place your right hand on her rib cage and help direct her landing and, if necessary, assist her flight. Remember to hang on to the gymnast's left arm until she has landed with balance because round-off dismount sometimes produces a lot of momentum away from the end of the beam.

Common errors:

1. Failing to kick legs and hips up in a vertical line over the hands.
2. Bending the elbows before landing.

Variation: A cartwheel dismount is a similar movement, but it involves a greater risk of damage to the knees from lateral force than the round-off. For this reason alone many teachers postpone teaching the cartwheel until the gymnast is in a team, where she can get more individual attention.

SAMPLE ROUTINES

As soon as a gymnast knows two or three movements, start having her combine the movements into a routine. Performing even short routines helps the gymnast think of balance beam movements as a unit. It also reminds her that balance beam is not a slow moving balance performance but rather a flowing, rhythmic event with dynamic qualities. Below are several short routines that you might find helpful.

Routine 1

1. Straight-arm support mount about 3 feet from the end of the beam. Finish the mount facing the long part of the beam.
2. V-sit; swing legs back.
3. Knee scale; step forward to a stand.
4. Standing pivot turn.
5. Two steps back.
6. Squat jump to squat.
7. Squat pivot turn.
8. Pirouette dismount.

Routine 2

1. Fence mount to stand in middle of beam.
2. Standing pivot turn.
3. Croisé pose.
4. One dip step.
5. One chassé.
6. Squat pivot turn to stand.
7. Step, stride leap.
8. Step, single-legged squat.

9. Roll back—roll up (lead-up for rolls).

10. Roll up to straddle seat; swing legs back to knee scale.

11. Fence dismount.

Routine 3

1. Squat mount in middle of the beam.

2. Quarter squat pivot turn to stand.

3. Two dip walks.

4. Standing pivot turn.

5. Front scale pose.

6. Squat and prepare for forward roll.

7. Forward roll to V-sit.

8. Cross right leg under left on top of beam.

9. Rock forward and place weight on left foot; pose balanced on left foot and right lower leg.

10. Sit back down and perform back roll to knee scale.

11. Fence dismount.

11

Trampoline

Because trampolining is considered a high-risk activity, it is particularly important for you to carefully plan and control the trampoline's use. Guidelines for safe and prudent use of the trampoline have been set forth by AAHPERD (American Alliance for Health, Physical Education, Recreation and Dance). These standards reaffirm the need for close supervision, skillful instruction, and the omission of the sommersault from class situations. When the sommersault is performed in teams and clubs, a spotting belt is appropriate. The avoidance of the sommersault in trampoline work is in response to a number of catastrophic (paraplegic or quadriplegic) injuries resulting from the movement.

Among the more general rules for trampoline use are:

1. Stop the bounce before preparing to leave the trampoline.
2. Climb off, don't jump off the trampoline.
3. Only one gymnast on the trampoline at a time.
4. Avoid bouncing too high or too long.
5. All four sides of the trampoline must be spotted at all times.

Because the trampoline involves high risk, it must be stored more securely when not in use. Besides being folded, the trampoline should be locked by chain if possible and kept in a locked room (preferably not the gymnasium). Many injuries occur during opening and closing the trampoline, so check the trampoline manufacturer's instructions for specific precautions.

The following movements are presented in order of increasing complexity. If the movements are learned in the order presented, prerequisite movements will be mastered before the more difficult skills that have specific prerequisites. Although not all of the movements have specific prequisites, it is still wise to learn them in order from simple to advanced.

BOUNCE AND KILL

Bounce

1. Start in the center of the trampoline.
2. Keep bounce low. Bounce only 4–8 inches off the bed.
3. Focus eyes on the trampoline frame pads.
4. Arms go up as you ascend and go down as you descend. The hands should always be kept within your peripheral vision. If your arms are allowed to extend behind your body (out of sight), it becomes more difficult to balance.
5. Bounce with feet apart.
6. In the air, the feet should be brought together, with the ankles plantar flexed (toes pointed).

Note: The foot coordination is difficult for some beginners.

Common errors: Off-balance or uncentered bounce. Typical causes are:

1. Failing to focus eyes on the trampoline frame.
2. Arms traveling behind the body.
3. Excessive height of bounce—this accentuates minor balance problems.

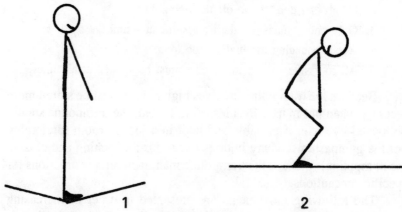

Figure 11-1
Killing the Bounce

Kill

As the bed is lifting, place hands on thighs, bend knees, and absorb the lift from the bed (Figure 11-1).

Note: The kill must be learned before proceeding to any other skills. It is the gymnast's solution to out-of-control bouncing and a vital safety precaution.

JOGGING AND MOGUL RIDING

Jogging

Run in place on the center of the trampoline. This helps to familiarize the gymnast with the trampoline and also benefits cardiovascular fitness.

Mogul Riding

Place feet about shoulder width apart on the center of the trampoline. Keep shoulders level while alternately depressing and releasing the bed. Feet remain in contact with the bed at all times. Increase the speed of the depressions until the motion resembles skiing over closely spaced bumps, or bouncing with feet glued to trampoline. The movement also helps to familiarize the gymnast with the trampoline as it conditions the legs.

QUADRANT BOUNCING

The bounce-and-kill learned above accentuates in-balance bouncing. A bounce on the trampoline from any spot except the center tends to throw the gymnast toward the center, off balance. Quadrant bouncing teaches the gymnast how to return to balance following such off-balance bounces.

1. Designate each quadrant of the trampoline with a number.
2. Using low bounces, bounce from quadrant to quadrant in a specified order. Initially the bounces should stay within 1 foot of the center.

THE HALF TWIST–180°

After ascending from the bed, twist and land facing the opposite direction, with balance and on the red X.

Combinations: Half twist between each quadrant in quadrant bouncing.

BASIC DROP 1: SEAT DROP

Each of the basic drops should be tried by assuming the landing position on a still trampoline before trying it from a stand or bounce. So sit on center of bed, legs together and extended forward with knees straight. Place hands on the bed by the hips, fingers pointing toward the toes.

After trying the seat drop on a still trampoline, take a few low bounces. At the height of a bounce pike, lift the legs to horizontal with knees straight and land in center of bed. As the bed lifts after the seat drop, lift arms forward and upward. Extend the hips and contact bed in a standing position.

Common Errors

Symptom: Heels or hips hitting first.

Correction: Pike more aggressively or less aggressively.

Symptom: Difficulty returning to a standing, erect position.

Typical causes:

1. Forgetting to place hands on the bed by hips with fingers pointing toward toes
2. Insufficient contraction of the hip extensors such as the gluteal group

Useful corrections: Lean farther forward from the hips while in the seat drop.

Combinations

Bed contacts are in italic:

1. *Seat drop,* half twist, *bounce* (good lead-up for swivel hips).
2. *Bounce,* half twist, *seat drop* (good lead-up for swivel hips).
3. Swivel hips (*seat drop,* half twist, *seat drop*).

Perfect combinations 1 and 2 above, then try to combine 1 and 2 with the addition of a standing bounce between them. The sequence will be *seat drop,* half twist, *bounce, seat drop.* If this combination is successful and *if* the body is straight (hips) during the twist, then attempt the same combination without the extra bounce. So, *seat drop,* half twist, *seat drop.*

Common error: Failing to extend hips during twist.

Teaching cues: "Feet follow center red line during twist."

TUCK JUMP

As the bed lifts during a regular bounce, tuck the legs and momentarily clasp them with your hands. Land in a regular, erect bounce.

DUTCH (STRADDLE) JUMP

As the bed lifts during a regular bounce, pike and straddle the legs. Extend the arms so that the hands touch the outside (lateral) portion of the ankles momentarily. Do *not* reach for the toes because doing so generally causes the ankles to dorsal flex. Land in a regular, erect bounce.

BASIC DROP 2: HAND-AND-KNEE DROP

The hand-and-knee drop is safer than a knee drop and it is an excellent lead-up for the front drop. Start on a still trampoline in a hand-and-knee drop position, knees behind the red line, hands in front (Figure 11-2).

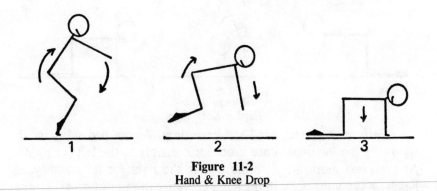

Figure 11-2
Hand & Knee Drop

Maintain the correct position while the spotters push on the bed simultaneously to produce a very small bounce. Concentrate on landing evenly in a correct hand-and-knee drop with each bounce. Then assume a standing position, take a very small bounce, lift hips, pike, lower chest and land in a correct hand-and-knee-drop position. Following the hand-and-knee drop, return to an erect bounce by lifting your head and shoulders, extending hips.

Common errors: Landing with too much weight on hands or knees.

Typical causes:

1. Failing to pike or lift hips.
2. Sitting back on heels instead of keeping knees at a right angle.

Combinations

1. Seat drop, hand-and-knee drop (Figure 11-3). As soon as the bed starts to lift following the seat drop, pull your torso close to your thighs.

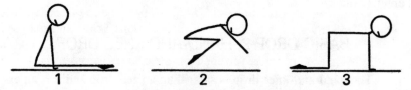

Figure 11-3
Seat Drop to Hand & Knee Drop

2. Hand-and knee-drop 180° turntable—a good lead-up to a front drop turntable (Figure 11-4).

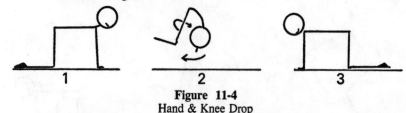

Figure 11-4
Hand & Knee Drop

Perform a correct hand-and-knee drop. As the bed starts to lift following the hand-and-knee drop, look sharply to the left (or right). At the same moment, push the bed to the right (or left) with your hands. Keep your body in the hand-and-knee drop position as it turns 180° to face the other end of the trampoline. Land in a hand-and-knee drop following the 180° turn.

Common Errors

Symptom: Incomplete turn.

Typical cause: Not forcefully pushing against the trampoline.

Symptom: Landing on the knees rather than the hands *and* knees during the second hand-and-knee drop.

Typical cause: Allowing the shoulders to lift from the horizontal position as the turn is made.

BASIC DROP 3: FRONT DROP

Note: The front drop must be carefully and slowly taught to avoid the gymnast landing either thighs or chest first rather than evenly—if this happens, she will usually go home with a sore back.

1. Lie down on the trampoline in a front-drop position (Figure 11-5). Do *not* tuck arms under the body or extend arms totally.

2. Assume the hand-and-knee drop position on a still trampoline. The spotters again produce a small bounce while you maintain a good hand-and-knee drop position. Select a good, even hand-and-knee drop and just before you contact the bed, extend your legs backward and your chest and arms forward.

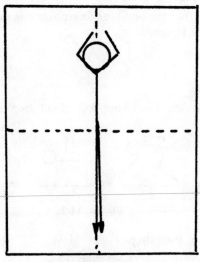

Figure 11-5
(Top View) Front Drop

3. Take a few, small standing bounces; land in a hand-and-knee drop; then as the bed lifts, extend into a front drop (Figure 11-6).

4. After you have mastered the previous three steps, repeat step 3, but this time do not actually land in the hand-and-knee drop. Instead, just an inch or two before you would contact the bed in a hand-and-knee drop, extend into a front drop. Remember to pass through a good hand-and-knee drop position in the air.

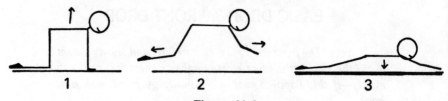

Figure 11-6
Hand & Knee Drop & Front Drop

Common Errors

Symptoms:

1. Landing with waist in front of center line.
2. Landing on chest or thighs first rather than waist first.

Typical causes:

1. Moving behind the center line to start the front drop causes the bed to propel the body forward and upward rather than only upward.

2. Omitting the hand-and-knee drop position in the air often results in a thigh-first landing.

Combinations

1. Seat drop, hand and knee drop, front drop (Figure 11-7).

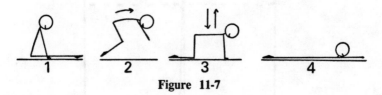

Figure 11-7

2. Seat drop, front drop (Figure 11-8).
3. Seat drop, straddle, front drop (Figure 11-9).
4. Turntable 180°.

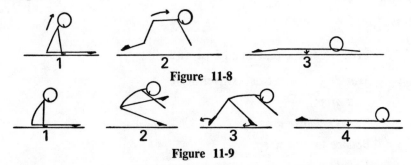

Figure 11-8

Figure 11-9

After mastering the hand-and-knee drop turntable, replace the first hand-and-knee drop with a front drop. Thus the sequence is front drop, half turn, hand-and-knee drop. Then replace the second hand-and-knee drop with another front drop so that the second sequence is front drop, half turn, front drop. Remember to stay in a tuck or hand-and-knee drop during the turn and then open up for the front drop.

ELEMENTARY ROUTINES

This is a good point in the development of trampoline movements to inject a few routines. If you choose to have your students make up their own routines, the following guidelines may be of help:

1. The routine should have a total of five (short), seven (medium) or 10 contacts, with a kill being required as the fifth, seventh, or tenth contact.

2. Preliminary bounces before the beginning of the routine are not counted.

3. The requirement of one or two changes of direction is useful in the seven and 10 contact routines.

Below are a few suggestions for routines for use as set, predetermined routines. Each contact is in italics.

Routine 1

Five bounces, one change of direction.

Seat drop

Bounce

Hand-and-knee drop

Half turn to *hand-and-knee drop* (hand-and-knee drop turntable)

Kill

Routine 2

Five bounces, one change of direction.

Seat drop to half twist (swivel hips).

Seat drop

Hand-and-knee drop

Bounce to tuck jump

Kill

Routine 3

Five bounces, two changes of direction.

Straddle jump; bring legs together in the air; land in a

Seat drop, straddle to

Front drop, half turn

Hand-and-knee drop, half turn

Hand-and-knee drop

Kill

Routine 4

Seven bounces, two changes of direction.

Tuck, jump, *bounce*

Half twist to *seat drop*

Hand-and-knee drop

Bounce

Seat drop, half twist (swivel hips)

Seat drop (swivel hips)

Kill

BASIC DROP 4: BACK DROP

It is a good idea to have the previous skills well mastered before moving to the fourth and final basic drop, the back drop.

Lie down on the back, with the waist in the center of the trampoline. Extend the legs vertically, with knees straight. Place hands on front part of thighs and lift head and tuck chin (Figure 11-10).

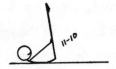

Figure 11-10
Back Drop Landing Position

From a standing position without any bounce, kick one leg up to a horizontal position or beyond. Join the first leg with the second. Drop the shoulder blades (scapula) down toward the bed at the same moment. Place hands on thighs and tuck head (Figure 11-11).

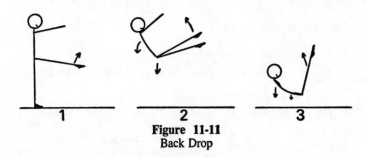

Figure 11-11
Back Drop

Teaching cues: "Make believe you are doing a drop kick with the first leg up."

Once a consistent, correct landing is mastered from a standing position, try the back drop from a small bounce, lifting both feet at the same time. Return to a standing position is effected by pushing the thighs away from the body as the bed begins to lift. At the same time gently thrust the hips forward and arch the back a little bit, lifting the hands overhead (Figure 11-11).

Teaching cue: Going over the imaginary fence indicated by the X's in Figure 11-12 is often effective in adding height to the process of getting to a stand.

Common Errors

Symptom: Whiplash type of situation as the body contacts the bed.

Typical cause: Failing to tuck the head.

Symptom: Hips contacting the bed rather than the back.

Typical cause: Failing to lift the legs to vertical.

Teaching cue: Insist that the hands be placed on the thighs.

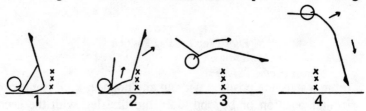

Figure 11-12
Back Drop to Standing Bounce

Combinations

Contacts are in italics.

1. *Back drop* to *hand-and-knee drop* (Figure 11-13).
2. *Back drop, hand-and-knee, front drop* (Figure 11-14).
3. *Back drop, front drop* (Figure 11-15).
4. *Hand-and-knee,* half twist, *back drop* (Figure 11-16).

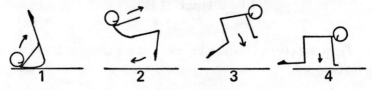

Figure 11-13

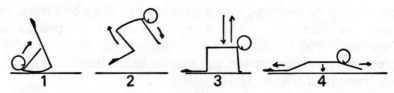

Figure 11-14

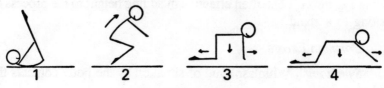

Figure 11-15

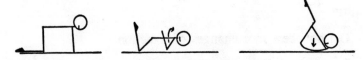

Figure 11-16

Note: As the bed lifts following the hand-and-knee drop, it is vital to keep the shoulders low and wait until a second hand-and-knee drop almost occurs before starting the twist by throwing one arm across the body.

5. *Seat drop, hand-and-knee drop,* half twist, *back drop.*

6. *Seat drop,* half twist, *back drop.*

Note: From the seat drop, proceed to a momentary hand-and-knee drop position and only at the last moment perform the twist and back drop.

7. *Back drop,* half twist, *back drop* (cradle).

Note: Once again, wait until the last moment before the twist is performed.

INTERMEDIATE ROUTINES

Contacts are in italics.

Routine 1

Ten bounces, four changes of direction.

Seat drop, half twist (swivel hips)

Seat drop (swivel hips)

Hand-and-knee drop, half twist

Back drop

Bounce

Seat drop

Front drop, half turn (turntable)

Front drop (turntable)

Bounce, half twist

Kill

Routine 2

Ten bounces, four changes of direction.

Front drop, half turn (turntable)

Front drop (turntable)

Hand-and-knee drop

Bounce, tuck jump

Bounce, half twist

Seat drop, half twist (swivel hips)

Seat drop (swivel hips)

Bounce

Back drop, half twist

Kill

In conclusion, let us review several overriding teaching principles for the trampoline:

1. A higher bounce does *not* correct mechanical errors. So teach and practice with a low bounce.

2. Demonstrate with a low bounce. Otherwise the observing gymnast begins to believe that the joy of the trampoline comes from height rather than perfection of movements.

3. Religiously adhere to the safety guidelines.

12

Evaluation and grading in gymnastics programs

An evaluation scheme, to be effective in a gymnastics setting, should:

1. Encourage practice rather than terminate interest in the movement tested.
2. Differentiate between skill levels in the performance of specific movements rather than only determining if the gymnast can perform them.
3. Be usable with an ease of administration.
4. Evaluate cognitive understanding of mechanics, spotting, common errors, and so on.
5. Offer the evaluative mode of testing movements in a routine rather than only individually.
6. Not be based on one attempt.
7. Allow for individual preferences or expertise in various events.
8. Be progressive rather than forcing the gymnasts to perform difficult movements before mastering the prerequisites.
9. Allow provision for considering improvement and effort if desired.
10. Allow for variations in testing requirements to account for individual differences in back flexibility and so on.
11. Convert easily to a numerical score for grading.

The following examples meet many of the above criteria. However, they are presented for illustration only because an evaluative scheme must also take into account your particular class size, age level, time schedule, equipment availability, and so forth. Hopefully, these examples will provide ideas with which you can create a perfect evaluation scheme.

If you use an evaluative scheme similar to Example 1, (p. 198) you might want to consider the following:

1. Have your gymnasts complete the requirements for a C before moving on to those for the B.

2. Allow your gymnasts to ask to be checked off on items when they are ready during the scheduled testing time. If they are not successful with a specific movement, suggest they practice and try again later.

3. Use a broad, yellow felt-tipped pen to simply color the items which each gymnast has checked off. The use of a yellow felt pen allows you and the gymnast to see at a glance what is remaining to be accomplished.

4. Put the requirements on a ditto and reserve one for each gymnast.

Example 2 involves a smaller number of movements, but each movement performed is given a numerical grade rather than being checked off. As the gymnast improves, allow her to perform the movement again. If her performance is better, raise her score, but if her performance has declined, don't reduce her score. To reduce her score would act as a bar to the motivation to practice. You can have one gymnast perform the same movement right after the previous gymnast because the gymnast need not make any choices. (See p. 201.)

Stunts and self-testing activities (Chapter 5) lend themselves easily to self- or group check-offs. These movements are usually presented to a class early in the gymnastics unit when the students are often still getting to know each other. Grouping five to ten students together either homo- or hetrogeneously to perform and check off the stunts helps develop trust and helpfulness among your students.

However, tumbling and other gymnastics movements do not lend themselves to this approach because there is no opportunity for you to provide corrective comments about form or mechanical errors.

Example 3 is a sample chart for groups to check off stunts and self-testing activities. (See p. 202.)

Routines

Putting gymnastics movements together into a routine increases their complexity and is helpful in developing an appreciation for competitive gymnastics. Most coaches seem to feel that there is a point reached when the *members* of a new gymnastics program become *gym-*

nasts. The incorporation of complete routines, even rudimentary ones, as soon as possible helps to speed the process of building gymnasts.

There are two types of gymnastics routines: compulsory and optional. Compulsory routines are predetermined by a person other than the individual gymnast. All gymnasts in a given group perform identical routines. On the other hand, optional routines are created by the individual gymnast (sometimes with the assistance of her coach) to meet her own creative and movement talents.

Any type of routine is difficult for the beginner to learn, but compulsories at least establish a pattern and help solve the problem of self-consciousness. It also obligates the gymnast to establish a repertoire of basic movements that would often go ignored in favor of the generally more interesting optional work.

If your class or club includes a wide range of skill levels, you might find it helpful to construct your compulsory routines with choices. The gymnast who has perfected a more difficult movement than her peers can, if she chooses, replace a related, simpler movement in the routine. Let's use a compulsory routine on the unevens for an example of how this works.

1. Facing the high bar, mount with a straight-arm support mount on the low bar. *Option*: back hip pullover mount.
2. Swan. *Option*: back hip circle.
3. Single-leg cut. *Option*: single-leg shoot-through.
4. *Option*: leg circle.
5. Single-leg cut into a sitting position on the low bar, facing the high bar.
6. Skin the cat.
7. Quarter turn in preparation for performing a single-leg pullover to the high bar. *Option*: double-leg stem rise.
8. Skin the snake dismount.

For the beginner, the opportunity to learn one routine and then simply slip in more advanced movements as they are mastered is quite helpful. For the teacher attempting to grade routines, the compulsory basis of the routine provides a foundation of expectations for the routine. The addition of the more difficult options into a more advanced student's routine is easily accommodated into the grading system. For each option performed in the basic routine, give the gymnast 0.5 additional points on her routine's score (1–10 points). Another alternative for adjusting the score of the gymnast who performs the more difficult routine is to reserve 2.5 points out of the possible 10 in a routine for difficult options. So a gymnast who performs a basic routine perfectly would receive 7.5 points out of a possible 10. Similarly a gymnast who performs her routine with one option added perfectly would receive a score of 8.0.

Minimeets

The experience gained from participation in some type of competition is generally both an incentive and a boost to the gymnast's appetite for work. Try a minimeet in your class. Divide the class into two or three teams that are somewhat equal in skill (that is, a few of your more highly skilled gymnasts on each team, and so forth). Have one performer from each team perform a routine. After one gymnast from each team has completed her performance, have the class or selected group from the class rank the two or three performances from 1—best; 2—middle; and 3—third. Keep track of which team receives the 1, 2, and 3. Repeat the process with another two or three gymnasts. The winning team is the team with the fewest points.

If you conduct your minimeet with only two teams, identify each with a color (for example, red and green). Have your student judging panel simply raise the color flag of the team whose routine they thought was the best of the two shown.

Demonstrations

A culminating activity toward which a gymnastics class can strive is a demonstration for parents, community, or even another school that does not yet have a gymnastics program. Whatever method you select to evaluate or culminate your students' gymnastics experience in any given time period, remember to include a healthy dose of fun.

EXAMPLE 1

The following criteria will be used to determine 75% of your grade for the skill section of this course. The other 25% of the skill section will be determined by your routine performance selected from floor exercise, balance beam, and uneven parallel bars. Remember that your skill grade accounts for 45% of your final grade. The rest of your final grade is made up of the following: written examinations—40%, effort and improvement—5%; attire, attendance—5%; spotting ability, willingness to move equipment, attitude—5%.

For a C	For a B	For an A
Tuck forward roll to pose	All of C requirements	All of B and C requirements
Handstand w/ light spot	Good cartwheel	Super cartwheel
Cartwheel	3 more from Column 1	Handstand forward roll
Any backward roll	1. _____	1 more from Column 1
Handstand forward roll w/ spot	2. _____	1. _____
Skin the cat w/ light spot	3. _____	2 more from Column 2
Swan on high bar	3 more from Column 2	1. _____
Forward roll on high bar w/ half twist	1. _____	2. _____
Perfect seat drop	2. _____	
2 different turns on beam	3. _____	
1 leap or jump on the beam	2 more from Column 3	
1 pose on the beam	1. _____	
(See p. 200.)		
	2. _____	

Plus 5 others from Column 1
  1. _____
  2. _____
  3. _____
  4. _____
  5. _____
Plus 3 others from Column 2
  1. _____
  2. _____
  3. _____
Plus 3 others from Column 3
(one of which must be a vaulting skill)
  1. _____
  2. _____
  3. _____

Column 1	Column 2	Column 3
Half-straddle forward roll	Back hip pullover	Beam—foward roll
Full scale forward roll	Thigh roll	w/spot
Back tuck roll	Skin the cat without spot	Beam—front kick turn
Back half straddle roll 1	Leg circle (light spot)	Beam—pivot turn
Back half straddle roll 2	Back hip circle (light spot)	Beam—squat pivot turn
Straddle back roll	Leg circle without spot	Beam—back kick turn
Headstand	Back hip circle without	Beam—series of 2
Handstand—3 seconds	spot	leaps on jumps
Handstand to bridge	Hand-and-knee drop	Courage mount
Tripod, sit-stand and	Half twist to seat drop	Squat mount
around the world	Seat drop to half twist	Squat vault
Egg sit—10 sec.,	Swivel hips	Flank vault
tip-up—3 sec., and	Hand-and-knee turntable	Front vault
tangle		Stoop mount
Stride leap, cat leap, and		
hitch kick		

EXAMPLE 2

0–10 points possible on each requirement
10 = Perfect

NAME

	Handstand forward roll (Max. 5 pts. if spotted)	Cartwheel	Back hip circle (Max. 5 pts. if spotted)	Leg Circle (Max. 5 pts. if spotted)	Stem rise or single-leg pullover	Fence mount on beam	Forward roll on beam (Max. 5 pts. if spotted)	Squat vault	Flank vault	Swivel hips	Floor or beam routine

90–100 = A
80– 89 = B
70– 79 = C
60– 69 = 0

EXAMPLE 3

Stunts

Egg sit—10 seconds								
V-sit—10 seconds								
Sit-stand								
Tangle								
Around the world								
Jump and slap heels—10×								
180° jump-twist—3 w/balance								
360° jump-twist—3 w/balance								
Bells—3 on each side								
8-person merry-go-round (up)								
8-person merry-go-round (down)								
Back-to-back get up								
Chest stand—base								
Chest stand—top								
Angel balance—base								
Angel balance—top								

☒—Attempted

■—Perfected

Names

Index